Eisenman Architects
university of Phoenix stadium for the Arizona Cardinals

MN 725.827 EI84P 2008

Eisenman
  Architects/University of

Knowlton School of Architecture
The Ohio State University

Source Books in Architecture 8
Todd Gannon, Series Editor

# Eisenman Architects/ University of Phoenix Stadium for the Arizona Cardinals

Princeton Architectural Press, New York

Published by
Princeton Architectural Press
37 East Seventh Street
New York, New York 10003

For a free catalog of books, call 1.800.722.6657.
Visit our web site at www.papress.com.

© 2008 Princeton Architectural Press
All rights reserved
Printed and bound in Canada
11 10 09 08  4 3 2 1 First edition

No part of this book may be used or reproduced in any manner without written permission from the publisher, except in the context of reviews.

Every reasonable attempt has been made to identify owners of copyright. Errors or omissions will be corrected in subsequent editions.

Design: Juliette Cezzar / e.a.d.

Special thanks to: Nettie Aljian, Sara Bader, Dorothy Ball, Nicola Bednarek, Janet Behning, Becca Casbon, Penny (Yuen Pik) Chu, Russell Fernandez, Pete Fitzpatrick, Wendy Fuller, Jan Haux, Clare Jacobson, Aileen Kwun, Nancy Eklund Later, Linda Lee, Laurie Manfra, Katharine Myers, Lauren Nelson Packard, Jennifer Thompson, Arnoud Verhaeghe, Paul Wagner, Joseph Weston, and Deb Wood of Princeton Architectural Press —Kevin C. Lippert, publisher

Library of Congress Cataloging-in-Publication Data available upon request from the publisher.

## contents

- 10   Foreword: Excellence in Civic Architecture
  John Meunier

- 18   Chronology

- 22   Introduction
  Eisenman Architects

- 26   Preliminary Design

- 50   Cardinals History

- 60   Design Development

- 76   Construction Documents

- 92   Construction

- 122   The Stadium

- 142   When the Big Red Team Takes the Field
  Jeffrey Kipnis

- 158   Project Credits

## source books in Architecture

Following the example of music publication, Source Books in Architecture offers an alternative to the traditional architectural monograph. If one is interested in hearing music, he or she simply purchases the desired recording. If, however, one wishes to study a particular piece in greater depth, it is possible to purchase the score—the written code that more clearly elucidates the structure, organization, and creative process that brings the work into being. This series is offered in the same spirit. Each Source Book focuses on a single work by a particular architect or a special topic in contemporary architecture. The work is documented with sketches, models, renderings, working drawings, and photographs at a level of detail that allows complete and careful study of the project from its conception to the completion of design and construction. The graphic component is accompanied by commentary from the architect and critics that further explores both the technical and cultural content of the work in question.

Source Books in Architecture was conceived by Jeffrey Kipnis and Robert Livesey and is the product of the Herbert Baumer seminars, a series of interactions between students and seminal practitioners at the Knowlton School of Architecture at The Ohio State University. After a significant amount of research on distinguished architects, students lead a discussion that encourages those architects to reveal their architectural motivations and techniques. The students record and transcribe these meetings, which become the basis of these Source Books.

The seminars are made possible by a generous bequest from Herbert Herndon Baumer. Educated at the Ecole des Beaux-Arts, Baumer was a professor in the Department of Architecture at The Ohio State University from 1922 to 1956. He had a dual career as a distinguished design professor who inspired many students and as a noted architect who designed several buildings at The Ohio State University and other Ohio colleges.

Other Source Books in Architecture:

Morphosis/Diamond Ranch High School
The Light Construction Reader
Bernard Tschumi/Zénith de Rouen
UN Studio/Erasmus Bridge
Steven Holl/Simmons Hall
Mack Scogin Merrill Elam Architects/Knowlton Hall
Zaha Hadid/BMW Central Building

## acknowledgments

Developing this book with Eisenman Architects has been a pleasure. I thank Peter Eisenman, Richard Rosson, Cynthia Davidson, and Mathew Ford for their cooperation and conversation, and in Cynthia's case, for her gentle prodding to keep the rest of us moving. Of course the endeavor would not have been possible without the vision of the Arizona Cardinals. Bill Bidwill, Michael Bidwill, and Michael Rushman in particular deserve special mention.

Robert Livesey, former director of the Knowlton School of Architecture, remains a key ally of Source Books in Architecture. His enthusiasm and guidance are essential to the series' success. Jean-Michel Guldmann, interim director of the school, and Ashley Schafer, head of the architecture section, have also provided generous support. As always, Jeff Kipnis warrants special mention for his unwavering encouragement and support.

John McMorrough organized Peter Eisenman's Baumer lectures at the KSA and developed early drafts of the material. Linda Lee and Kevin Lippert at Princeton Architectural Press saw the book through production with their trademark efficiency and Juliette Cezzar provided thoughtful and energetic design.

Finally, I would like to recognize the innumerable contributions of Vi Schaaf. Since its inception, Vi has overseen the often complicated and always thankless financial aspects of this series with cheerful efficiency and sardonic wit. — **Todd Gannon**

# Foreword: Excellence in Civic Architecture
John Meunier

Throughout the history of great cities, certain buildings have been particularly significant, whether government structures—palaces, parliaments, or capitols—places of worship—temples, mosques, or cathedrals—or venues for theater and music—the open amphitheaters of Greece and Rome, the grand opera houses of Paris and Milan, the Burgtheater of Vienna, and the National Theatre of London. They not only housed their respective activities but were also symbols of the highest levels of achievement. Through their quality the architecture made a claim for excellence on behalf of their city. No Greek city was complete without its stadium, and our Olympic games are descended from those enacted centuries ago in the stadium of Olympia. The Colosseum in Rome is clearly an ancestor of today's modern stadium.

I commend the Arizona Cardinals, the city of Glendale, Arizona, the metropolitan community of Greater Phoenix, and the state of Arizona for their commitment to do more than construct a state-of-the-art sports facility. The building of this stadium for the Arizona Cardinals has been a huge challenge that has consumed a mountain of resources and talent, and we are witness now to how far they have gone in meeting that challenge. This new stadium creates a work of architecture that is an adequate symbol of the ambitions of this community to achieve eminence among the emerging great cities of the twenty-first century.

How has this been done? Not through the expenditure of great riches—this is not a luxurious building. In fact, it has one of the more modest budgets among its peers. Not by harking back to some fictional golden age of culture or athletic

achievement by hanging off its structure the trappings of nostalgia. This is not a building clad in a classical suit of clothes or pretending to have been built at a time when rivets lent a kind of gritty muscularity to our sports arenas. No, it engages with the kind of architectural exploration that permitted the construction of the Guggenheim Museum Bilbao and lifted the tired Spanish port city into a place of architectural pilgrimage.

With the decision to hire Peter Eisenman and Eisenman Architects as the design architect, the Arizona Cardinals made an extraordinarily courageous "draft pick." Eisenman is not an architect who has built his career, or his renown, on designing sports stadia. Although he is a lifelong football fan—he once insisted that a visiting professor's job at The Ohio State University include the promise of seats for OSU football games—Eisenman has built his reputation as a leader of innovative and provocative architectural thought and design. In his writing and his designs, he has challenged almost every architectural cliché and replaced them with fresh and challenging propositions. This is not to say that he denies the importance of architectural history. He offers a fresh reading of the history of architecture and cities that informs much of his work, including the design of this remarkable stadium in a remarkable city.

# chronology

**August 31, 1997**
At the recommendation of Michael Rushman, Bill and Michael Bidwill meet with Peter Eisenman during the NFL football game between the Arizona Cardinals and Cincinnati Bengals to discuss the design for a new stadium in Arizona.

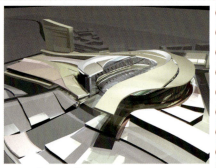

**March 1998**
A design for a multipurpose stadium in combination with a convention center and hotel is proposed for a site that spans the boundary between Tempe and Mesa.

**1997** **1998** **1999**

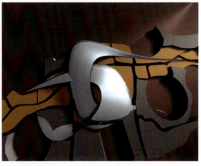

**October 1997**
Eisenman Architects begins work with the Bidwill family to develop a conceptual design for the new Arizona Cardinals stadium.

**November 1999:**
Governor's Advisory Task Force created.

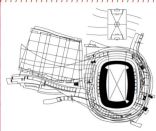

**May 18, 1999:**
A referendum to help fund Rio Salado Crossing, a 1,000-acre mixed-use development with the football stadium as its anchor, is rejected by the citizens of Mesa.

**January 6, 2001:**
AZSTA receives site proposals from 5 sites: Downtown Phoenix, Fort McDowell Indian Community, Tempe, Tempe/Mesa, and West Valley (Avondale).

**April 24, 2000:**
Arizona State Senate Bill 1220 passed, establishing the Arizona Tourism and Sports Authority (AZSTA).

**July 21, 2000:**
Authority holds its first meeting. James Grogan elected chairman. Other board members are appointed by the Governor, Speaker of the House, and Senate President.

**February 13, 2001:**
A site in Tempe, at the intersection of Washington Street and Priest Drive, is selected. Eisenman Architects develops a new design.

**September 5, 2000:**
AZSTA ratifies the Cardinals' selection of Hunt as the design-build contractor.

**August 02, 2001:**
In response to FAA concerns, the stadium is moved a little over 1,600 feet east of its planned site, and 600 feet south of the runway's center line, away from a new and previously undisclosed flight procedure.

2000 — 2001 — 2002

**November 28, 2000:**
HOK Sport retained as the Facility Architect

**November 7, 2000:**
Maricopa County voters approve Proposition 302 by a 52% to 48% vote, authorizing new tourism taxes and ratifying other elements of SB1220, which allows public funding for the construction of a new stadium

**November 14, 2001:**
AZSTA Board of Directors votes to begin the process of finding a backup site to the Tempe location after the FAA raises concerns about the stadium's proximity to the Phoenix Sky Harbor Airport. The design team analyzes a number of these potential sites.

**April 12, 2003:**
The Cardinals celebrate groundbreaking at the site of the future stadium in Glendale.

**August 29, 2002:**
The team and AZSTA agree to locate the new stadium in Glendale. Located at the interchange of Loop 101 and Bethany Home Road, just south of the new Glendale Coyotes Arena. Eisenman Architects begins a new, and final, design for the stadium.

**July 30, 2003:
site excavation begins.**

**August 27, 2004:**
The northeast supercolumn is topped off.

2002   2003   2004

**October 10, 2003:**
First concourse slab forms constructed.

**September 3, 2003:**
The first concrete columns are poured.

**August 1, 2004:**
Onsite assembly of the Brunel trusses begins.

**July 27, 2003:**
Project published by the New York Times for the second time.

**March 14, 2003:**
New stadium design unveiled to the public.

chronology

**February 17, 2005:**
Erection of upper-bowl precast risers is completed.

**June 1, 2006:**
Rolling field is moved into place for the first time.

**February 21, 2005:**
Stadium roof raised into place atop the supercolumns.

2005 — 2006 — 2007

**July 2005:**
Roof construction completed.

**August 12, 2006:**
Arizona Cardinals play first preseason NFL game in new stadium and defeat the reigning Super Bowl champion Pittsburgh Steelers by a score of 21 to 13.

# Introduction
Eisenman Architects

As American architecture has developed over the past two centuries, the idea of the town symbol has shifted from the steepled church to the courthouse, to the library, to the museum. Now the stadium, which has always been an important icon in American culture but not an object of high design, can be added to this list, as signature architects like Antoine Predock, who completed a baseball stadium for the San Diego Padres, and Arquitectonica, who designed a basketball arena for the Miami Heat, are getting major sport facility commissions in the United States.

In 1997, Eisenman Architects won the limited design competition for the Arizona Cardinals' new stadium in greater Phoenix. The Cardinals paired Eisenman with the sports division of HNTB, an architectural and engineering firm, to develop a high-design, iconic building for the Valley of the Sun.

For Eisenman, whose work largely centers on the relationship of the object—or building—to the ground, resulting in many "figured ground" projects, the stadium presented a new problem. Certain projects resist a figured-ground approach. For example, it is difficult to make a large theater for an audience of two or three thousand people without making some sort of object form, because the sheer size of the hall and its acoustic needs require a shape. A stadium similarly resists a figured-ground approach. Eisenman reframed the architectural problem to ask whether one could make a sport facility that denied the absolute symmetry that characterizes most arenas.

while it could be argued that any irregularity in the exterior shape of a building is not likely to reverberate on the inside of the building, Eisenman explored the possibilities for developing a dynamic interstitial space between the rectilinearity of the stadium's playing field and the nonsymmetrical exterior of the building. The interstitial zone was broadly defined here as the space between the playing field and the parking area and imagined as a sequence of spaces: from the parking lot to and through the skin of the building, through the space between the skin and the concourses, through the concourses themselves, and then finally to the seats overlooking the field. The problem then became how this sequence could operate architecturally while building a football stadium.

In the nine years between the original design competition and the completion and opening of the stadium in Glendale, Eisenman's conceptual approaches were applied in a number of different design proposals as a result of the the local politics that surrounded site selection. This book documents that process.

## preliminary design

# Preliminary Design: Tempe
## Eisenman Architects and HNTB, 1997–1998
## Tempe, Arizona

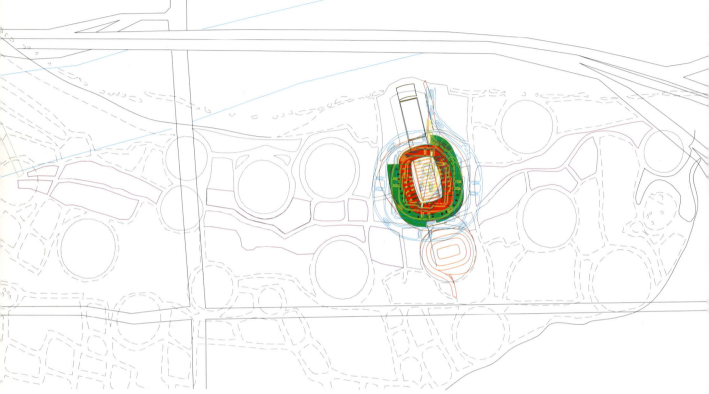

The first site was in the East Valley, near the Tempe home of the Cardinals' practice facility and the home of Arizona State University (ASU) and its Sun Devil Stadium, where the Cardinals had been playing since moving to Arizona from St. Louis. The first proposal included a hockey arena, football stadium, sports complex, a hotel, and shopping area. To meet the desire for something both modern and historical, Eisenman looked at the historic urban forms of the Hohokam Indian Nation, a community that had constructed ball courts for both recreational and sacrificial contests, and at symbolic forms seen in early Hopi sand painting. The particular mandala of the Hopi is the snake, which curls from its head to its tail but is an open-ended form. The snake is a symbol of life, of its beginning and its end.

The proposal had three key elements: the hockey arena, the football stadium, and a central hotel between them that would have contained some of the suites and club seats for the stadium and arena. The arena was abandoned, however, when ownership of the hockey team changed. The sports-center concept was discarded when East Valley mayors made it clear that any stadium project had to be about more than sports. They also felt that the project would be more likely to be approved if the local funding was shared between two communities, so the site was shifted slightly east to straddle the Tempe-Mesa border.

Preliminary Design: Tempe, 1997–1998

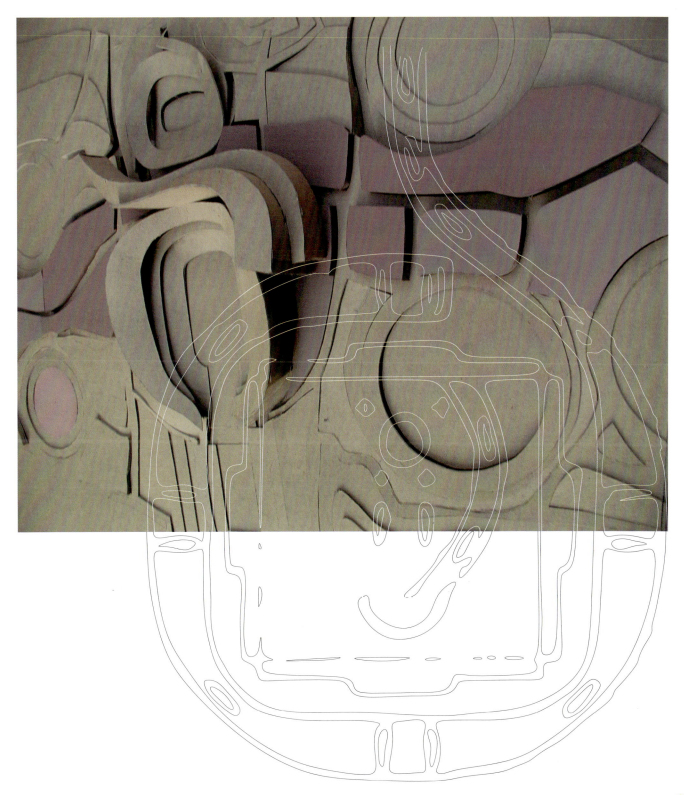

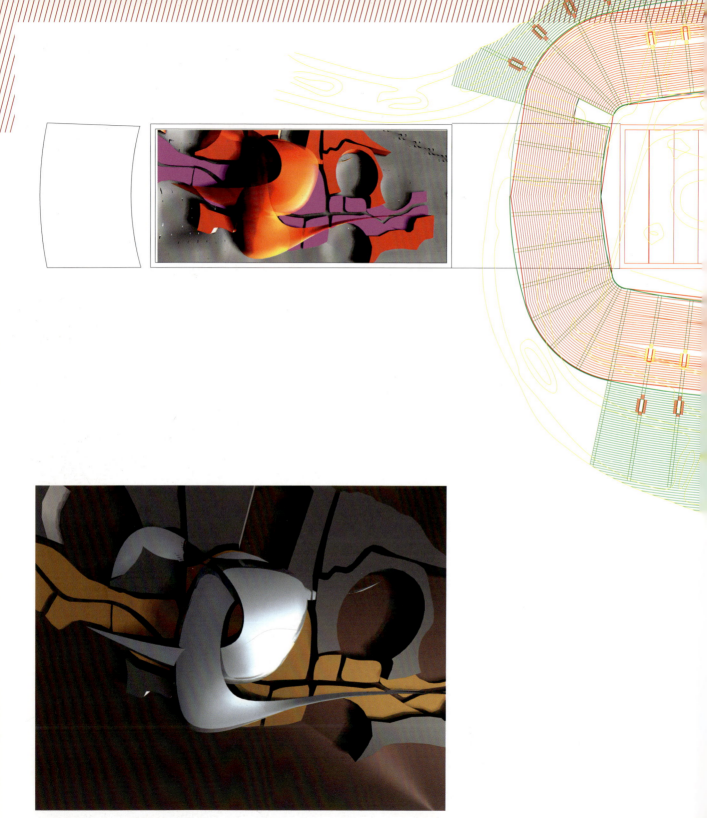

preliminary design: tempe, 1997–1998

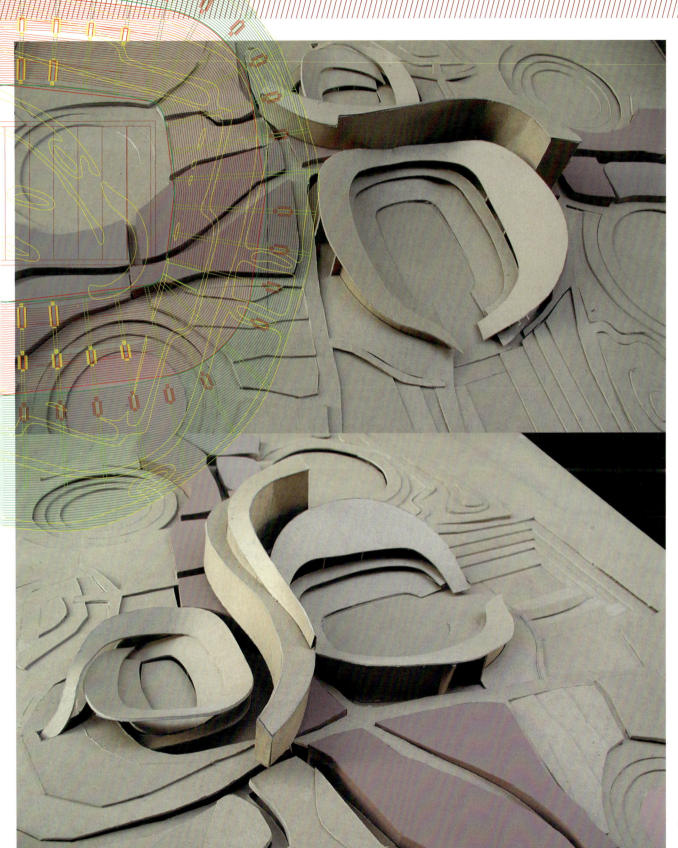

# Preliminary Design: Tempe/Mesa J.V.
## Eisenman Architects and HNTB, 1998–1999
## Tempe/Mesa, Arizona

The second project straddled the boundary between the cities of Mesa and Tempe and was combined with a convention center as a base—a kind of landform—from which a hotel and the stadium would rise up. It was imagined, in a way not fully understood at this juncture, that the playing field could move out of the stadium when there were no football games, thereby allowing the floor to serve as additional convention exhibitions space and the concourses as prefunction areas. Given the high cost of a new facility, the multipurpose potential of the stadium was central to all design schemes.

The Cardinals also wanted the atmosphere of an open-air stadium, even though it would need to be closed and air-conditioned on the hottest fall days. An operable roof, supported by two long-span trusses, and an open end, which allowed views out to the desert landscape behind one end zone, opened up an otherwise closed stadium to the outside. In addition, the design contained no vomitory to the seating bowl—the audience would always be in the space, never in a tunnel.

In this scheme Buro Happold began the structural design work by considering a variety of roof-framing options, which Eisenman wanted to be very light in appearance, even though they would be more than eight hundred feet long, and about ninety feet deep. The mandala form and "tail" of the first stadium proposal continued to be developed. The potential problem with a stadium that did not conform to a bilateral symmetry was that all of the quadrants, and thus all of the bays, were different. This was the basis of many discussions with the Hunt Construction Group, the contractors for the project, and added concerns about the possible extra costs brought by a nonsymmetrical stadium.

While the city leaders from Mesa and Tempe were quite enthusiastic about the proposal, the Tempe City Council refused to place a stadium resolution on the ballot for a public vote. The scheme was abandoned for lack of funding.

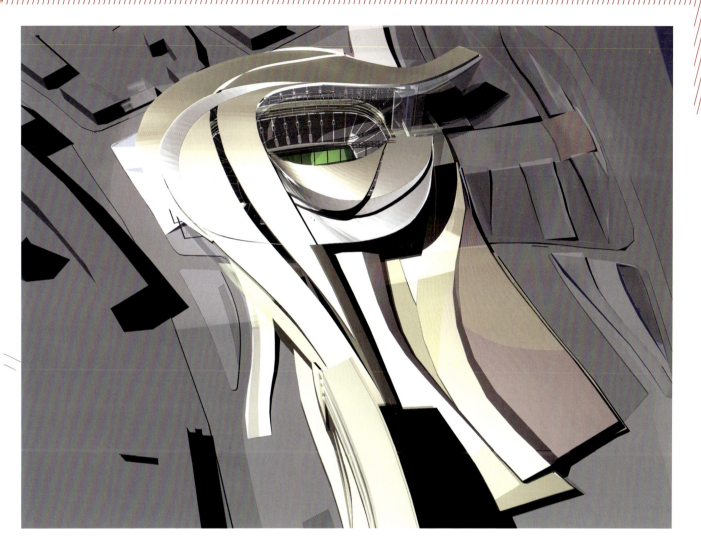
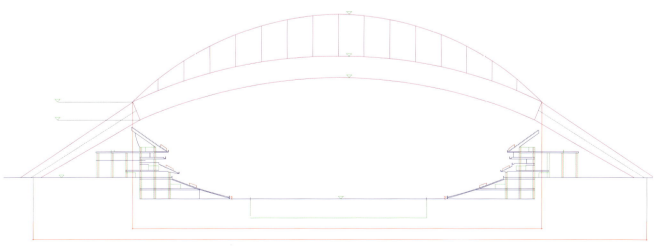

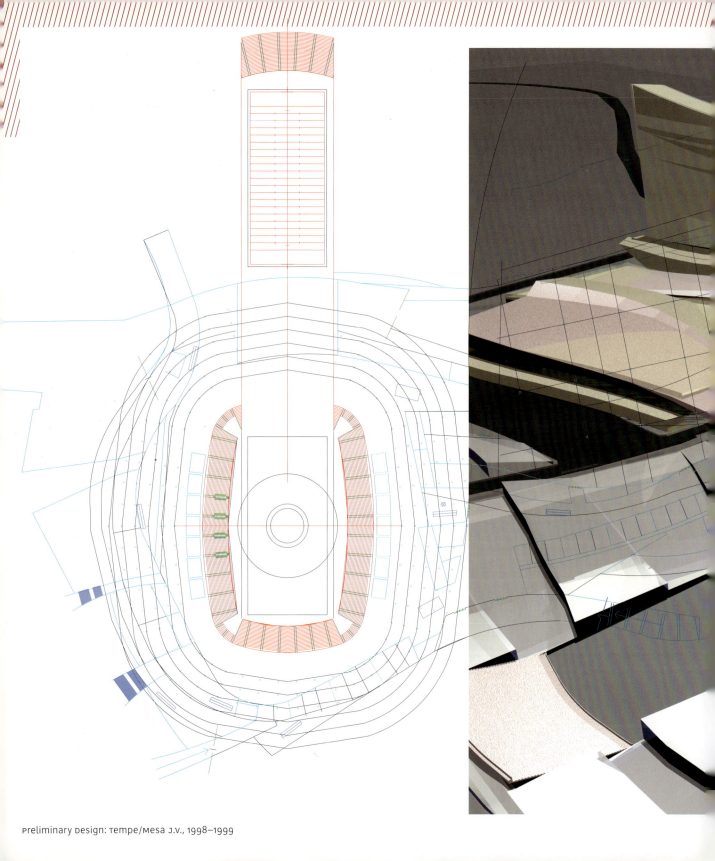

preliminary design: tempe/mesa j.v., 1998–1999

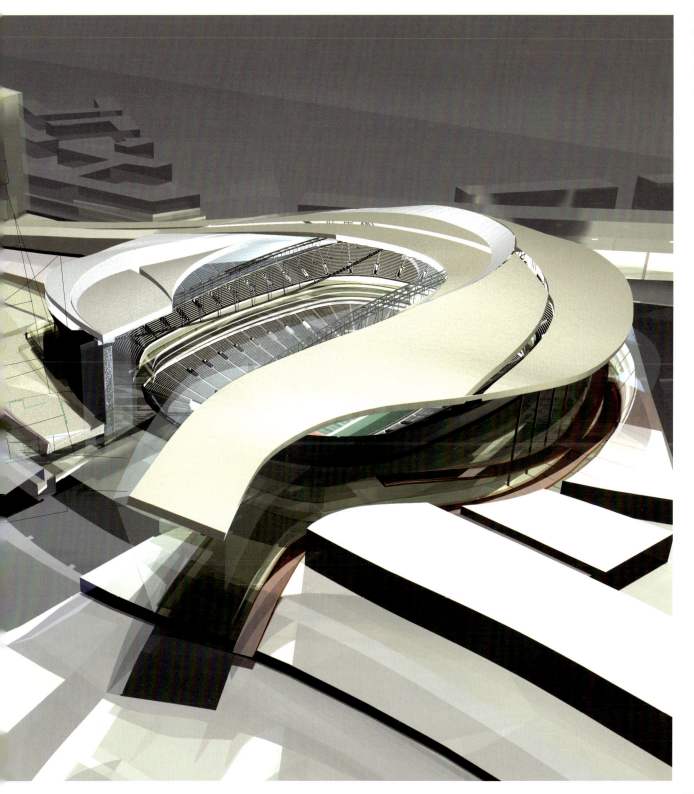

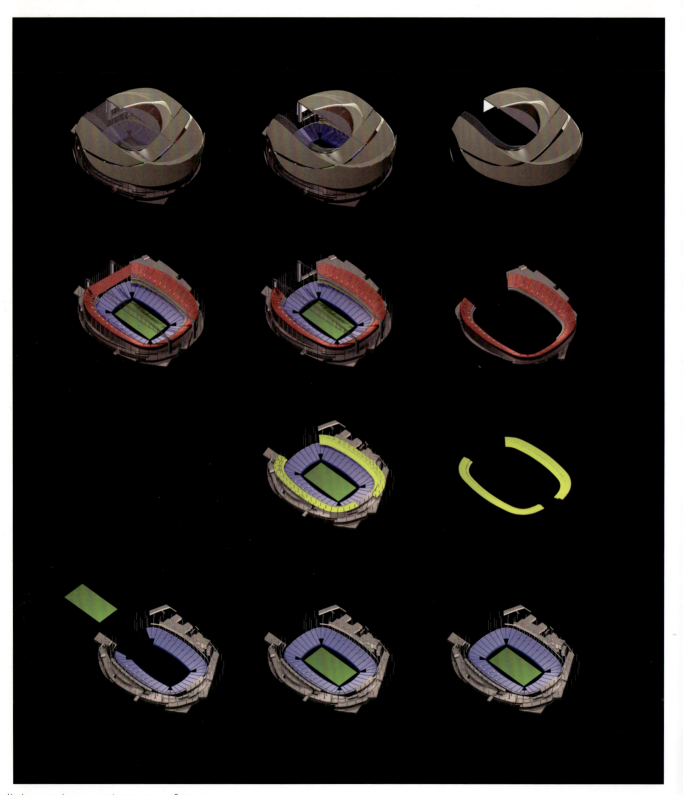

preliminary design: tempe/mesa j.v., 1998–1999

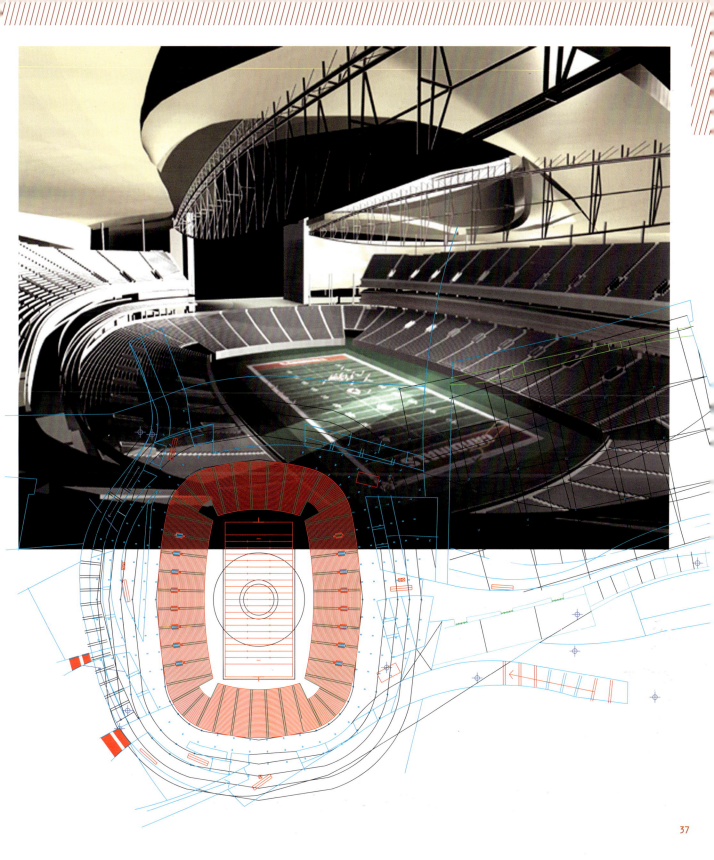

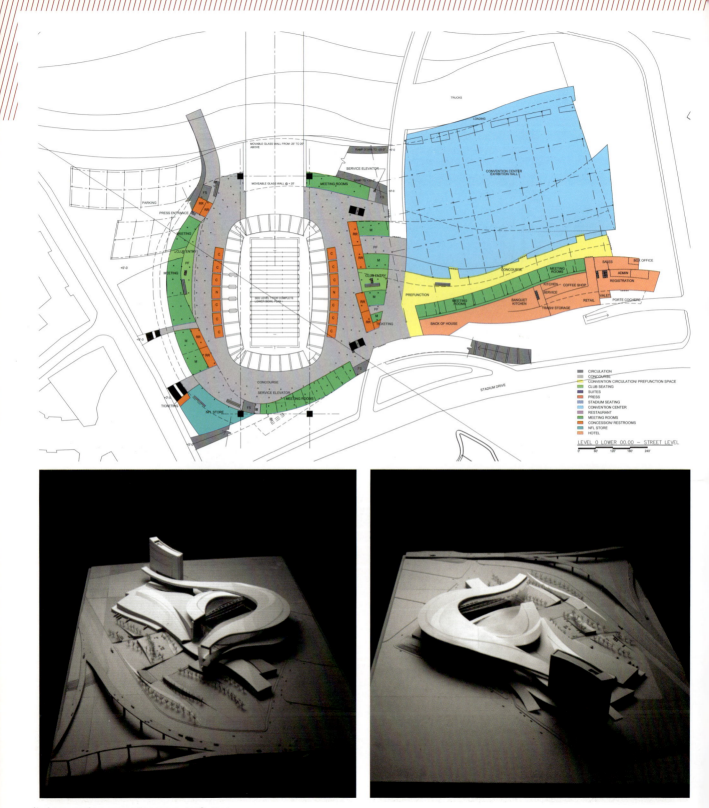

preliminary design: tempe/mesa j.v., 1998–1999

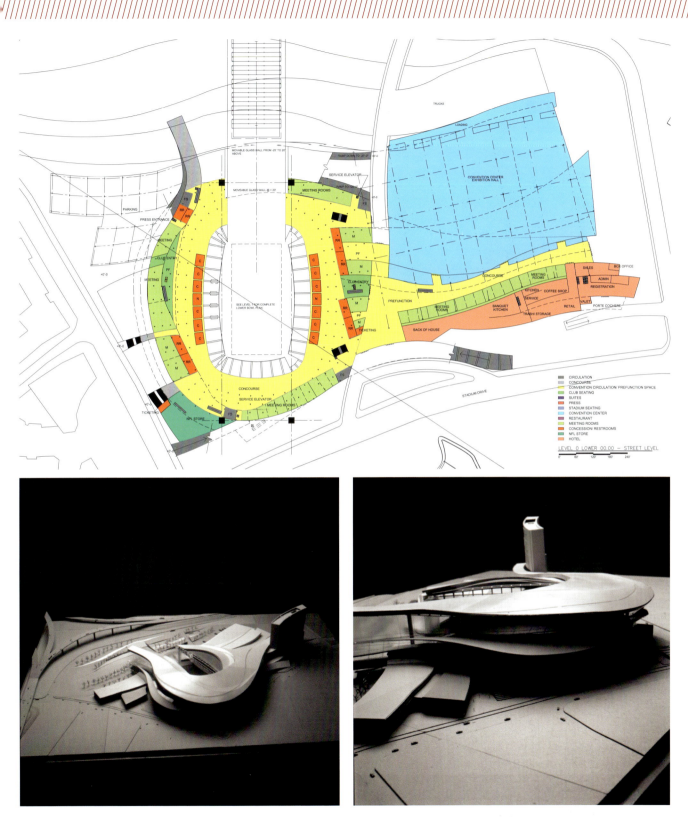

# preliminary design: rio salado crossing
## eisenman architects and HNTB, 1999
## mesa, arizona

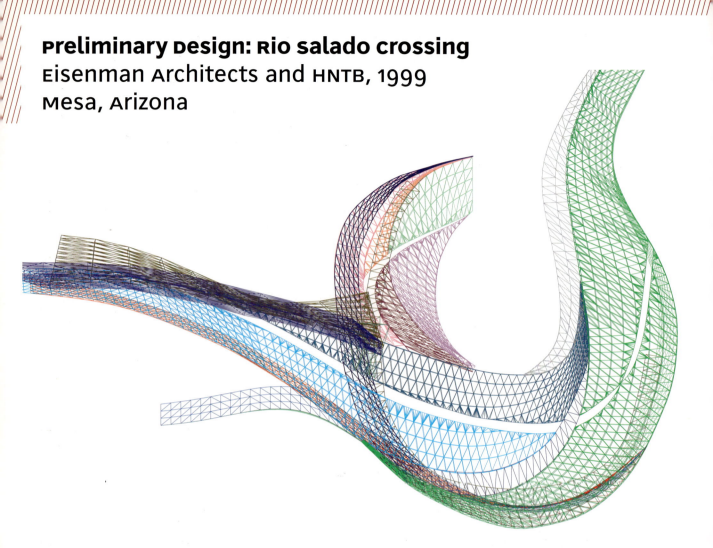

The Cardinals moved the project to a new site in Mesa proper, and Eisenman was given a new design problem including a stadium, a convention center, residential blocks, and a golf course. This was an enormous project. The stadium itself was re-sited almost intact from the Tempe-Mesa venture. Because of the mandala form, all of the exterior striations were horizontal—the articulation of the layers of transparent glass and opaque skin was horizontal. In addition, the top of the structure was ringed with glass to create the sensation of the roof being lifted off the facade enclosure. The citizens of Mesa had to vote on a bond issue that would allow revenues to be collected for the stadium, but the voters turned down the referendum. At that point the stadium appeared to be dead, and HNTB withdrew from the project.

preliminary design: rio salado crossing, 1999

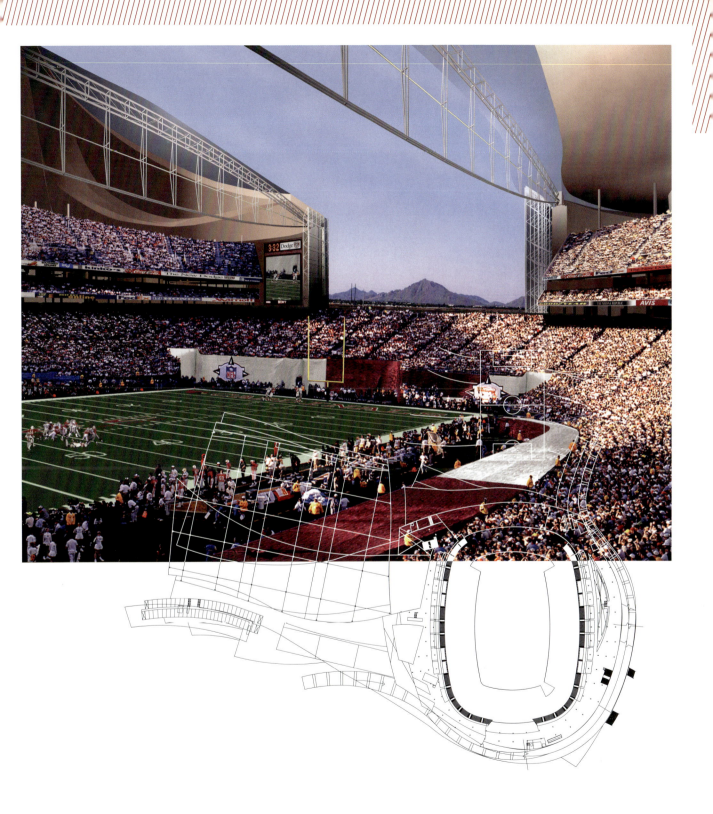

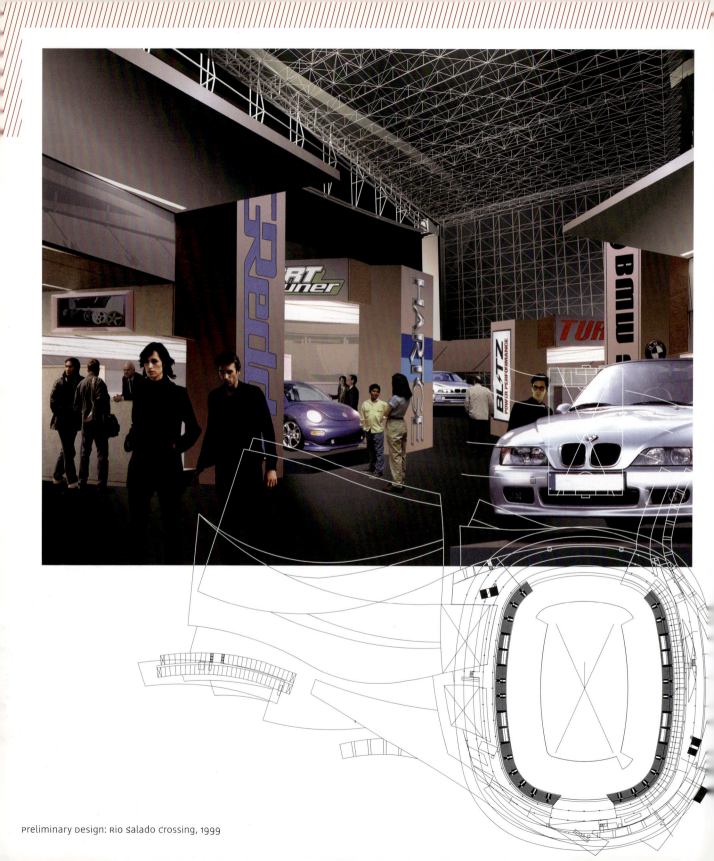

preliminary design: rio salado crossing, 1999

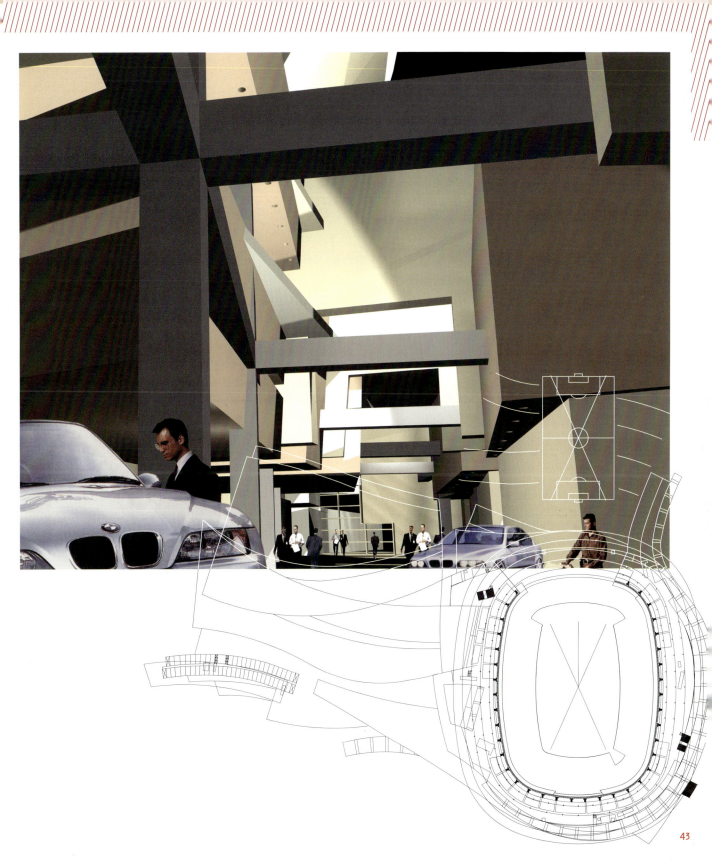

# preliminary design: papago park
## eisenman architects and HOK sport, 2000–2001
## mesa, arizona

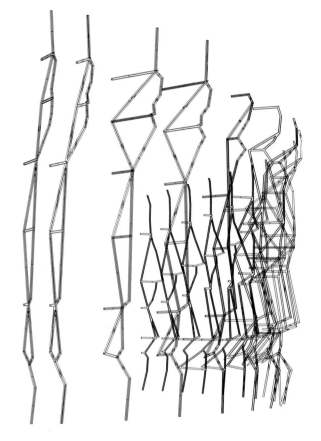

After the referendum defeat in Mesa, the state legislature voted to create a legislative entity called the Arizona Sport and Tourism Authority (AZSTA) to issue bonds in Maricopa County that would help to pay for the stadium, in addition to the money that the Cardinals owners would contribute. The project then moved to a new site back in Tempe, across the Rio Salado from Sun Devil Stadium. Hunt Construction asked HOK Sport in Kansas City to join the architectural team.

At Papago Park, Eisenman worked to keep the stadium's interstitial space intact, including all of the vertical circulation (stairs, ramps, and escalators), which was placed between the facade and the concrete structure of the seating bowl and concourse spaces. In the articulation of the secondary steel, some of the desired density was lost, including horizontal beams that were structurally unnecessary but were needed to bring down the scale of the space. The grid of horizontal and vertical elements was intended to play against the triangulated forms of the secondary steel.

Much of the energy in the original stadium proposals was lost when the project went back to Tempe. The new site was more constricted, and many of the previously proposed multipurpose aspects of the project had to be sacrificed. Some of the horizontal energy of the facade, the two Brunel trusses, and the open end remained, but the tail was diminished and now sheltered only the ramp to the upper concourse.

The city of Phoenix was concerned that the stadium was in the flight path to its Sky Harbor Airport—as are ASU's Sun Devil Stadium and the Diamondbacks' Chase Field. But it was now post–9/11. AZSTA made the policy decision that it would abide voluntarily if the FAA found that the stadium could be a possible hazard to air navigation. Even moving the structure to another parcel on the site failed to meet FAA requirements. By now, four years had been spent working on the project, but in hindsight, it was a fortunate ruling. This version of the stadium was the most symmetrical and objectlike of all of the proposed schemes.

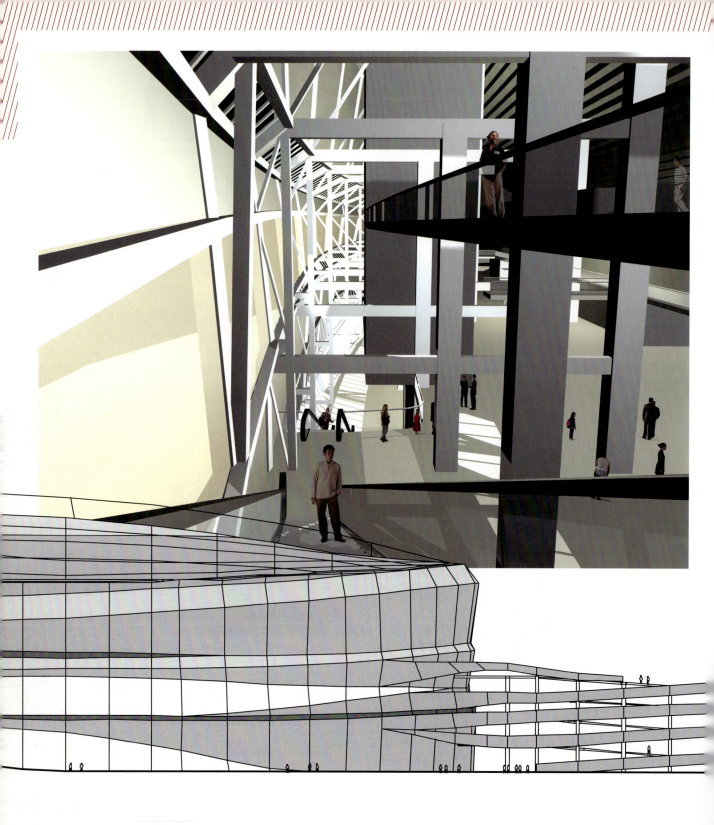
preliminary design: papago park, 2000–2001

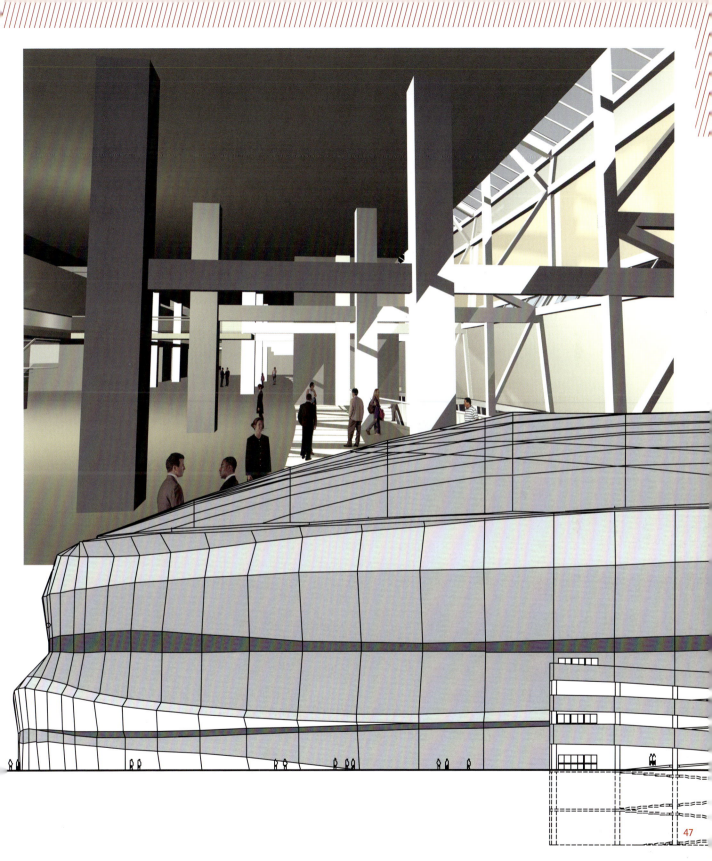

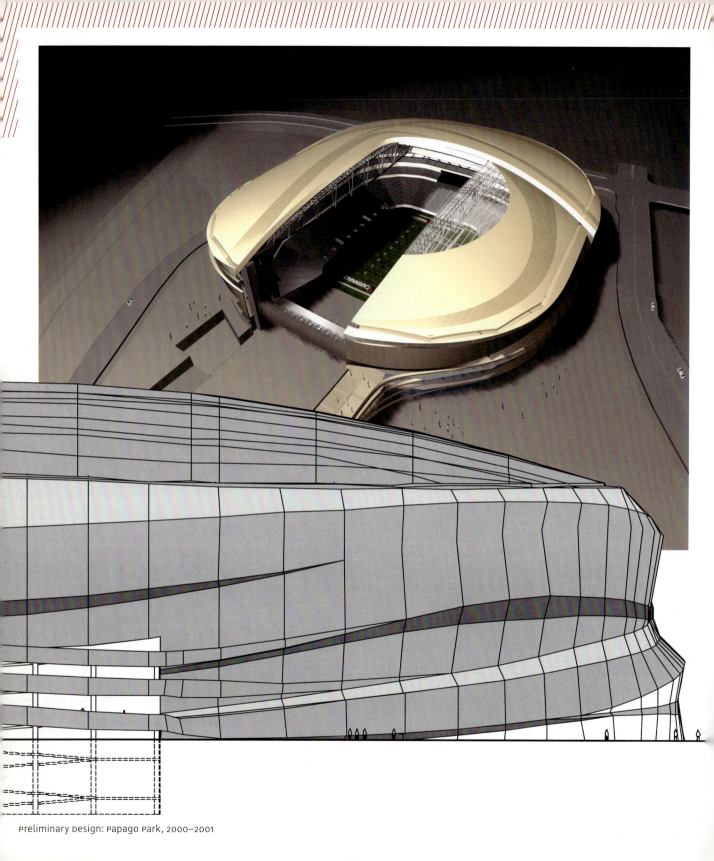

preliminary design: papago park, 2000–2001

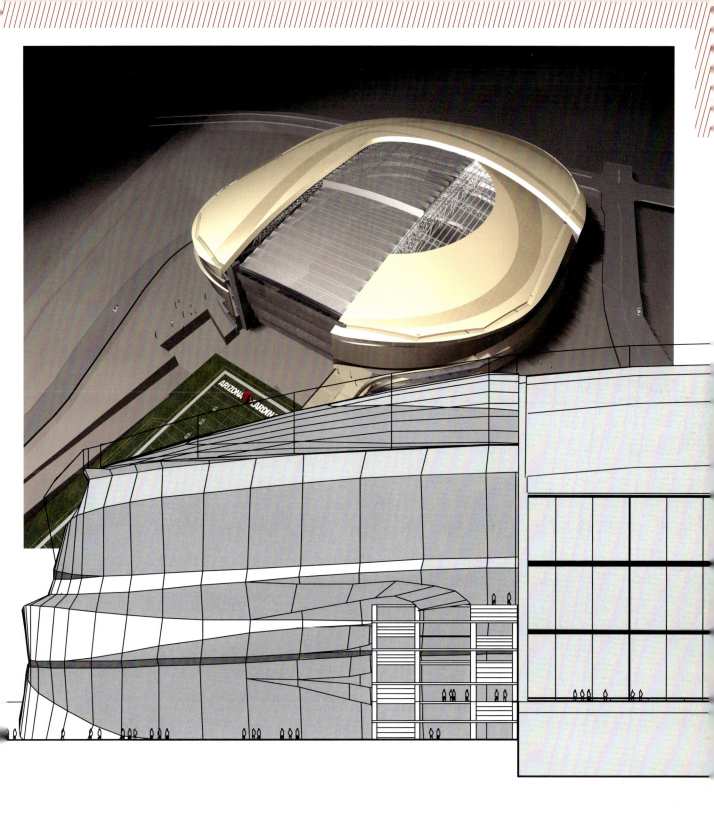

1900: cardinals' roots to neighborhood group to play football; predominant of chicago's

cardinals History

s trace their
: a neigh-
p gathered
all in a
y Irish area
outh side.

cardinals history

**Pre-1900**
Cardinals trace their roots to when a neighborhood group gathered to play football in a predominantly Irish area of Chicago's South Side, known as the Morgan Athletic Club, staging games whenever and wherever they could find an open field and interested fans, and wearing a large 'M' on their jerseys.

**1898**
Chris O'Brien, a painting and decorating contractor in the Chicago area, acquires the Morgan Athletic Club and changes its playing site to nearby Normal Field, prompting a new name—the Normals.

**1901**
The club gained its longstanding identification when O'Brien, finding a bargain, bought used jerseys from the nearby University of Chicago. The jerseys were a faded maroon color, prompting O'Brien to declare, "That's not maroon, it's Cardinal red!" The club's permanent nickname had been born.

The jersey color and location of the field—at the corner of Normal Boulevard and Racine Avenue—led to a new and obvious name, the Racine Cardinals.

**1920**
Racine Cardinals become one of 11 charter members of the American Professional Football League, forerunner of the National Football League, for the $100 franchise fee. Players wore leather helmets, numberless sweater jerseys, and earned a $40 paycheck.

**1922**
A team from Racine, Wisconsin, joined the NFL, prompting the Cardinals to change their name to the Chicago Cardinals. That year, the team also moved into their new home in Comiskey Park.

**1929**
O'Brien sells the team to Dr. David Jones, a Chicago physician, who lures Ernie Nevers out of retirement. On Thanksgiving Day, Nevers scores an NFL-record 40 points (six touchdowns, four extra points) in a historic 40-6 victory over the crosstown Chicago Bears. Nevers' feat remains the longest-standing record in NFL history.

**1932**
Charles W. Bidwill, then a vice-president of the Chicago Bears, purchases the Cardinals for Dr. David Jones's asking price of $50,000, and a new era begins.

**1947**
Charles Bidwill assembles a talented club that includes his "Dream Backfield" of Paul Christman at quarterback, Charlie Trippi and Elmer Angsman at halfback, Pat Harder at fullback, and Marshall Goldberg playing both offense and defense. Though Bidwill sadly passes away that spring and is unable to witness the fruits of his labor, Trippi leads the team to a 10-3 record, capped by a 28-21 win over the Philadelphia Eagles to be crowned NFL champions.

**1948**
Cardinals forge an 11-1 record and another berth in the NFL title game, only to be handed a 7-0 defeat by the Eagles in what became known as the "Blizzard Bowl."

**1960**
With the rival American Football League eyeing St. Louis as an expansion site, NFL owners vote unanimously to allow the Cardinals to relocate to St. Louis on March 13. The team would play home games in Sportsman's Park from 1960-65, then move into newly constructed Busch Stadium in 1966, adorned with their first helmet logo ever—a cardinal bird head.

**1974-75-76**
Head coach Don Coryell orchestrates a wide-open offense as the "Cardiac Cardinals," so named for their numerous last-minute comeback victories, record three consecutive 10-win seasons but are twice defeated in first-round playoff contests.

**1982**
Cardinals gain a berth in Super Bowl tournament in strike-shortened season with 5-4 record, but lose at Green Bay in first-round play.

**1988**
NFL owners vote on March 15 to allow the Cardinals, who have called St. Louis home for 28 years, to relocate to Arizona. The Phoenix Cardinals make Sun Devil Stadium on the campus of Arizona State University their temporary new home. Cardinals race to 7-4 record and share of the NFC East Division lead, but a rash of injuries result in a five-game losing streak to end the season and any chances for postseason play.

**1994**
Cardinals owner William Bidwill announces his intention on March 17 to change the name of the team to the Arizona Cardinals, which is adopted unanimously by a vote of NFL owners a week later.

cardinals history

### 1995-96
Cardinals serve as host team for Super Bowl XXX, played at Sun Devil Stadium.

### 1998
One of the NFL's youngest teams, the Cardinals end the franchise's 15-year playoff drought and earn a trip to the playoffs with a 9-7 record, then manage the club's first postseason victory since 1947 with a 20-7 victory over the Dallas Cowboys at Texas Stadium.

### 2000
On Election Day, November 7, voters in Maricopa County pass Proposition 302, the Tourism and Sports Initiative, to help fund a new stadium for the Cardinals, Fiesta Bowl, and future Super Bowls.

### 2003
The Arizona Super Bowl Committee wins bid on October 23 to host Super Bowl XLII in February, 2008 at the new Cardinals Stadium in Glendale, Arizona. Following an official groundbreaking on April 12, the first mass excavation at the site begins on July 30, with a completion target date of August, 2006.

### 2004
The Arizona Cardinals unveil a redesigned team logo, updating the classic cardinal head that has represented the team for 45 NFL seasons. Hall of Famer and former Cardinals player Larry Wilson said of the evolved logo, "It is absolutely fantastic. You see a lot of meanness and orneriness in this new logo and that is how you like to play the game. I have a lot of nostalgia for this game and the bird head, but to change with the times is important. Football is a nasty, mean game, and you should look that way when you take the field."

### 2006
On August 12, the Cardinals play their first preseason NFL game in their new stadium in Glendale, and defeat the reigning Super Bowl champion Pittsburgh Steelers by a score of 21 to 13.

On September 26, the stadium is officially named the University of Phoenix Stadium when the on-line educational institution buys the naming rights from the Cardinals.

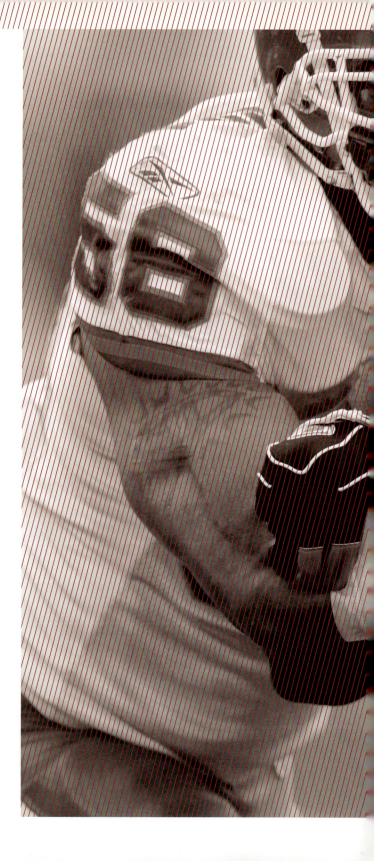

- **1.7 million** square footage of stadium
- **88** Total number of luxury lofts in stadium
- **7,501** Total number of club seats in stadium
- **7** Number of club lounges
- **63,400** Seating capacity for Cardinals games (expandable to 73,000 for Super Bowls and college Bowl games)
- **1,250** Approximate number of shade trees used throughout the stadium plaza
- **21** Number of vertical slots in the exterior wall of stadium
- **30** Height in feet of the giant numbers designating the three main entrances to the stadium
- **19** Width in inches of stadium seats; club seats are 21 inches
- **10** Number of elevators for public use in stadium
- **18** Number of escalators for public use in stadium
- **1,175** Total restroom fixtures for public use in the stadium (33 women's restrooms, 28 men's, and 12 family restrooms)
- **310** The number of fixed locations for fans to purchase food and beverages (does not include additional portable locations)
- **8,000** Tons of cooling used by the stadium's air conditioning
- **14,000** Number of on-site parking spaces (not including additional 11,000 on adjacent and nearby parcels)
- **15,451** Square footage of the Cardinals locker room area including equipment and training rooms, shower areas, etc. (Locker room itself is 5,000)
- **454,785** Votes in favor of Proposition 302 stadium legislation in 2000
- **1,218** Days between the stadium groundbreaking (4/12/03) and the inaugural game at the stadium (8/12/06)
- **16,340** Total number of jobs created by Proposition 302; overall economic impact is $1.95 billion
- **700** Average number of workers on site every day during stadium construction (3,000 total workers)
- **2.6 million** Total number of hours put in by workers during construction project
- **115+** Number of event days booked for first year at the stadium
- **1.1 million** Projected number of visitors to stadium in its first year
- **2/3/08** Date of Super Bowl XLII at University of Phoenix Stadium
- **2009** Stadium will host the Regionals of the NCAA men's basketball tournament.

Cardinals History

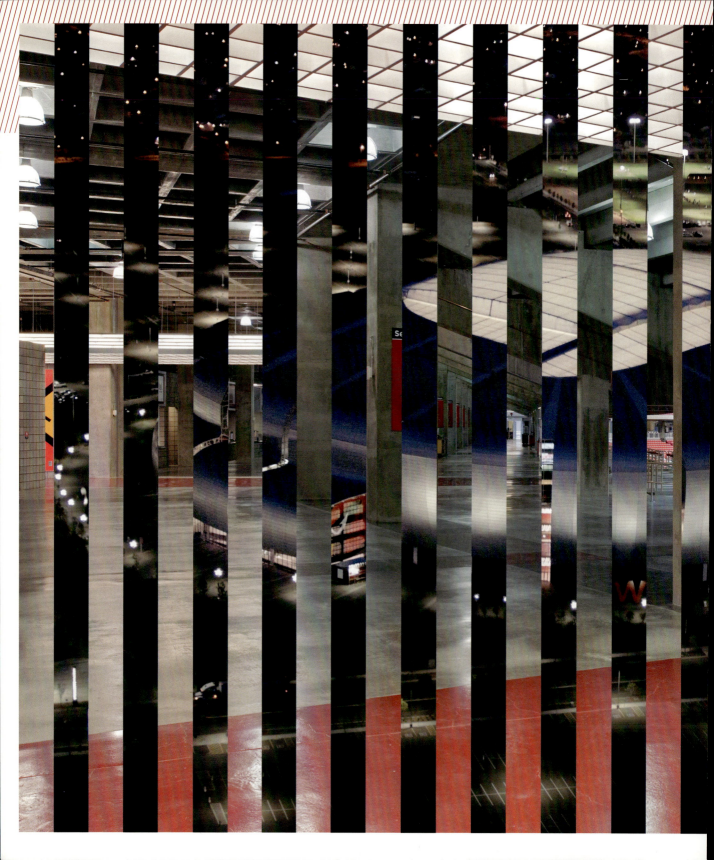

# design development

# design development: glendale
## eisenman architects and HOK sport, 2000–2001
## glendale, arizona

After exploring a variety of other sites in Maricopa County, including a site in downtown Phoenix and a site in the Gila River Indian Community, all of which were considered inappropriate for one reason or another, the Arizona Sports and Tourism Authority (AZSTA) selected a site in Glendale, in the west valley, only about a half-hour drive from Scottsdale and the airport. The Coyotes hockey arena (designed by HOK) was already being built in Glendale, and the addition of the Cardinals stadium would make this a preeminent sports destination.

Given the new location, the Cardinals requested a new design. It was important to rethink the design, which, after seven iterations, had been losing its initial energy. Certain design pieces could not be changed. The roof steel had been ordered for the project when the architects were working on Papago Park, and the schedule was so tight that the drawings for the seating bowl had to be followed. What could be addressed was the exterior appearance, which was altered from a shell with horizontal layering to one with glazed vertical cuts in the double-curved metal skin, thereby suggesting the striations of a barrel cactus. The next area of focus was on the interstitial spaces between the skin and structure. The panel system is a series of standard steel panels. Each panel has the capacity to undergo a little torque, and when put together, the torqued panels form a surface that curves in a very interesting way.

In an effort to avoid the prototypical sports stadium surrounded by a sea of asphalt-covered parking, the conceptual layers of the stadium were extended to the edge of the site. Stadium rays—registered in the roof—concourse floors, and plaza were run though the parking as landscaped, tree-covered walkways. Large striated islands of indigenous west valley plants interrupt the parking areas and provide a vast number and variety of spaces for tailgating.

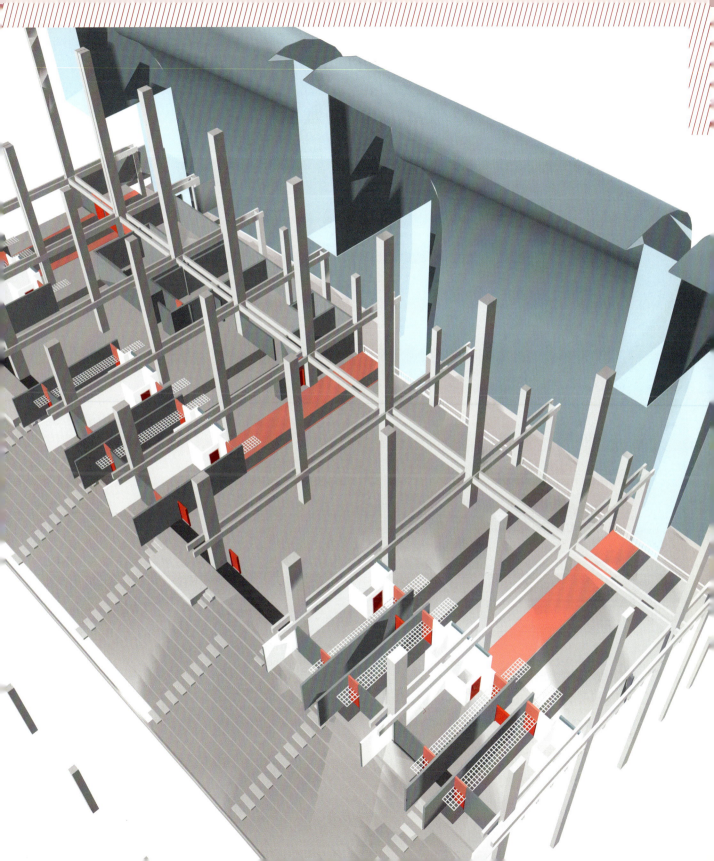

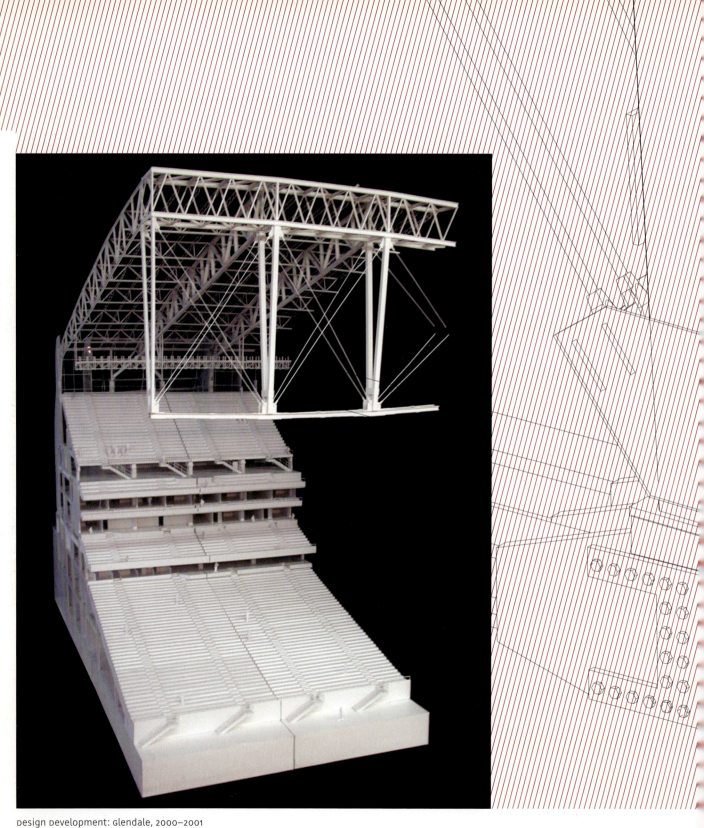

design development: glendale, 2000—2001

design development: glendale, 2000–2001

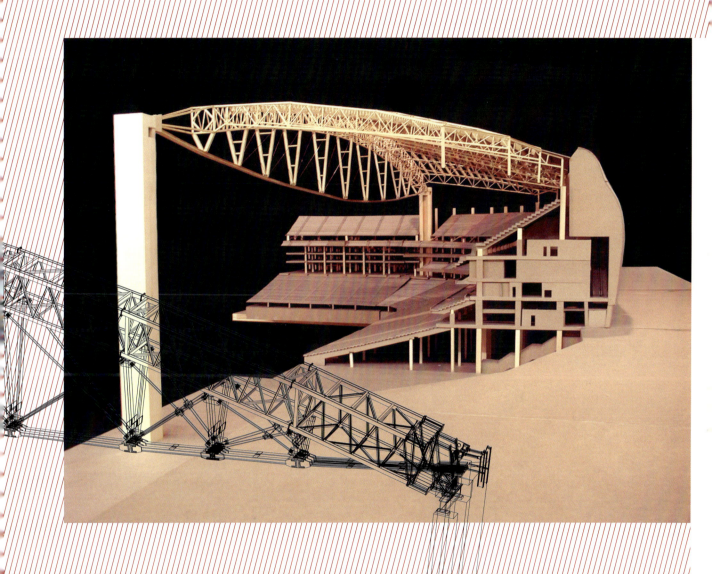

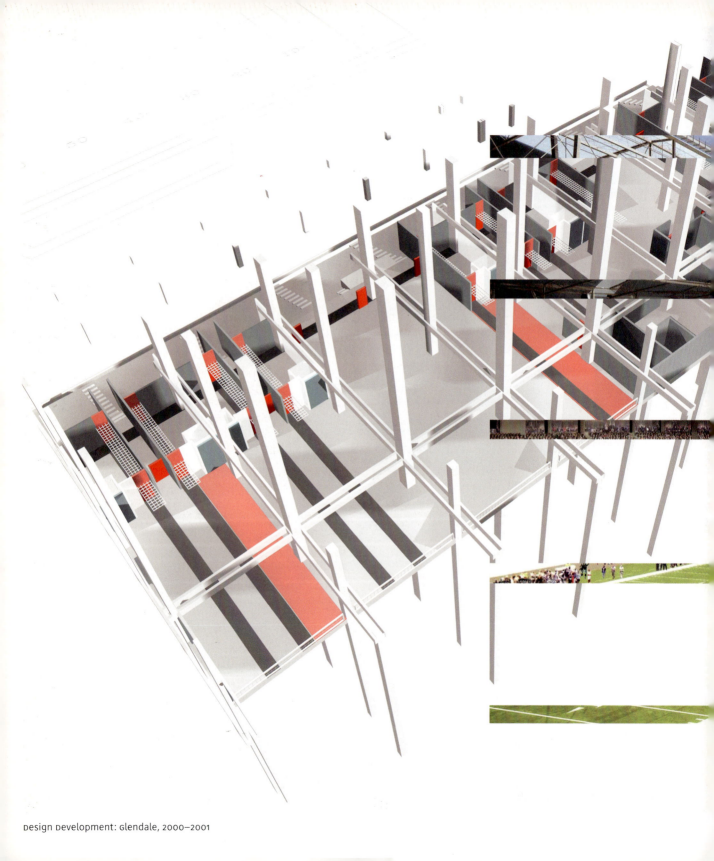

design development: glendale, 2000–2001

design development: glendale, 2000–2001

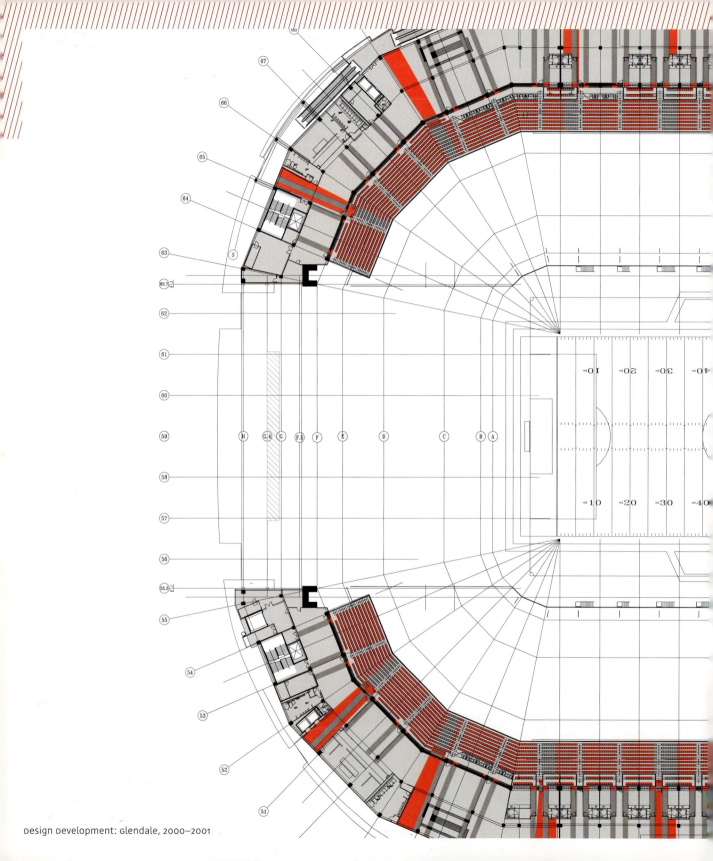

design development: glendale, 2000–2001

design development: glendale, 2000–2001

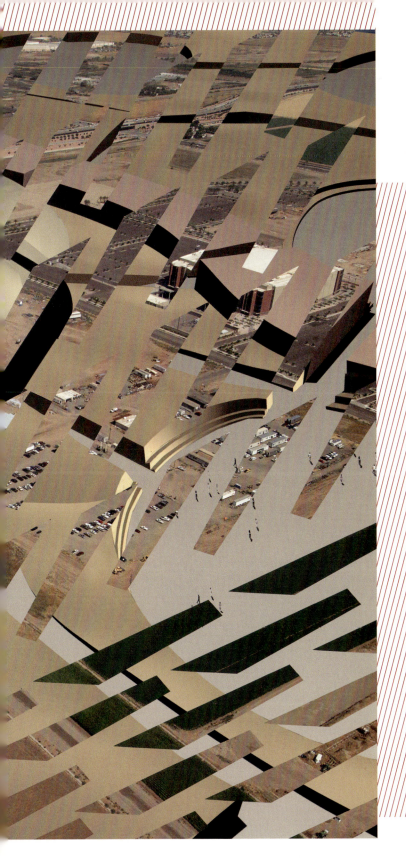

# construction documents

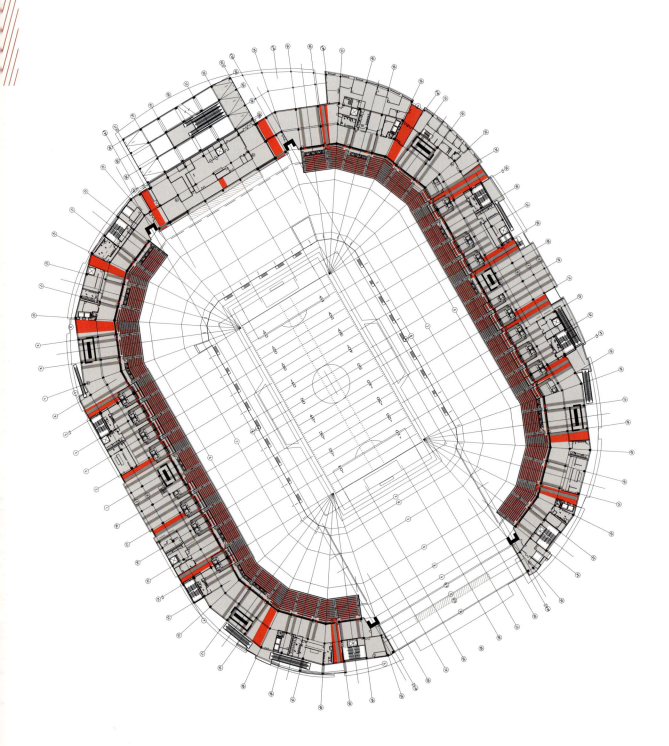

club floor + bars, 1:1800

construction documents

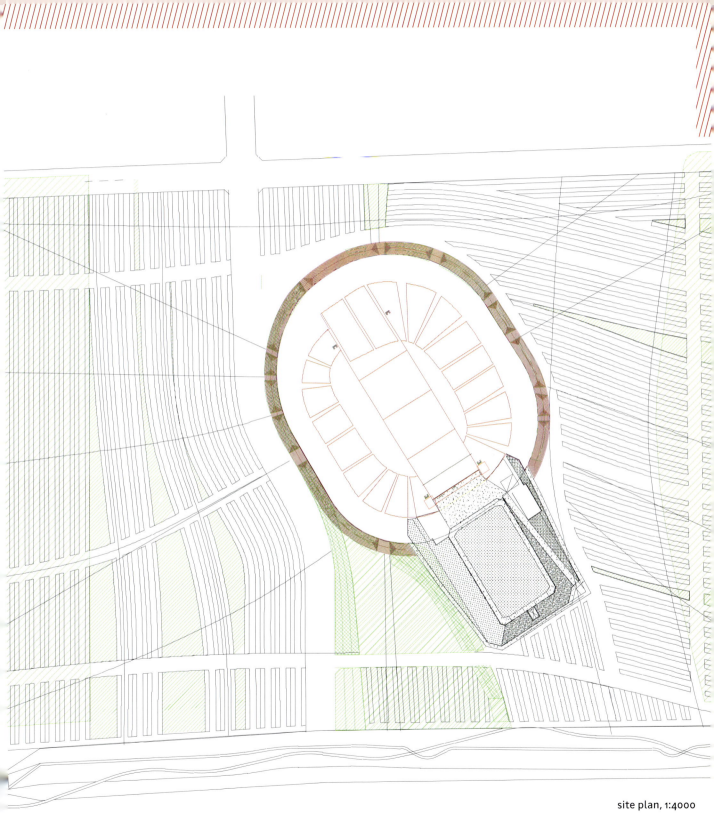

site plan, 1:4000

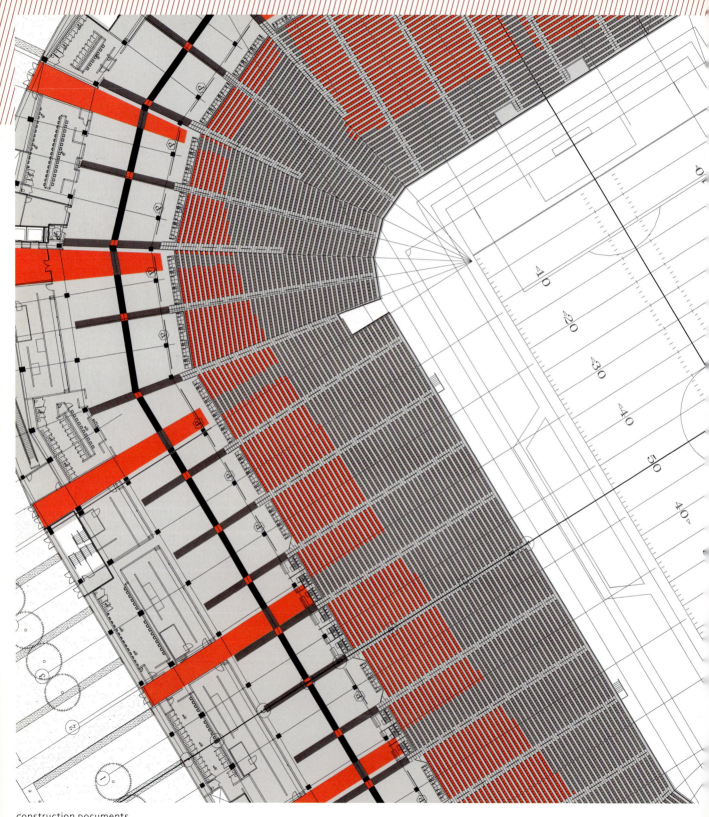

construction documents

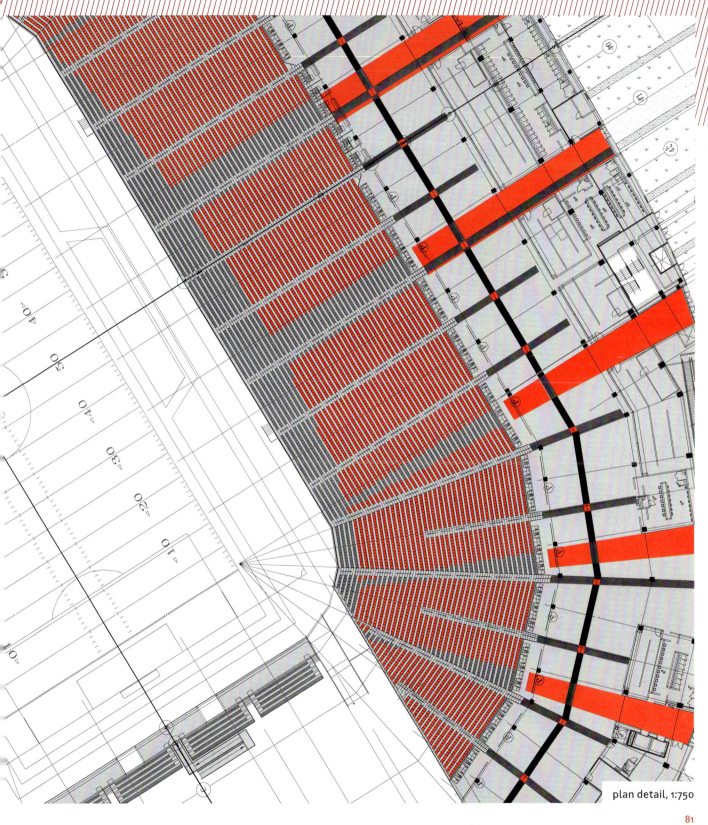

plan detail, 1:750

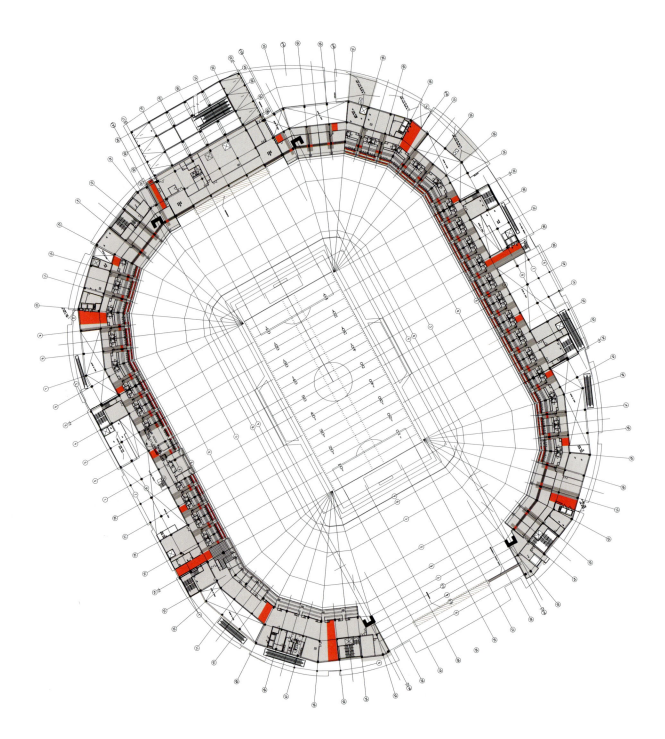

suite floor, 1:1800

construction documents

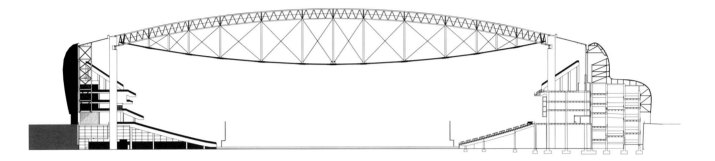

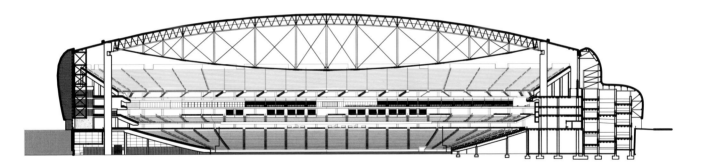

sections, 1:1800

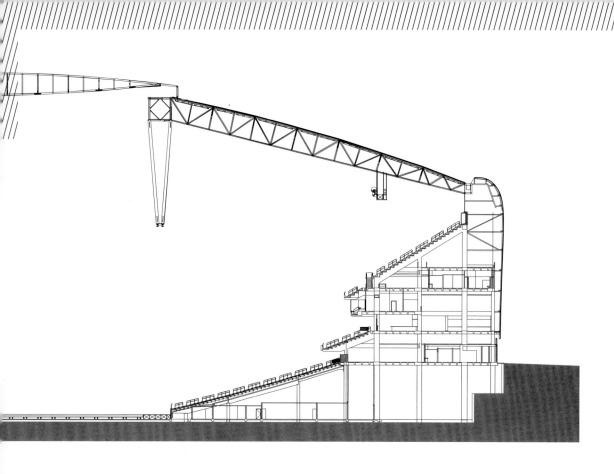
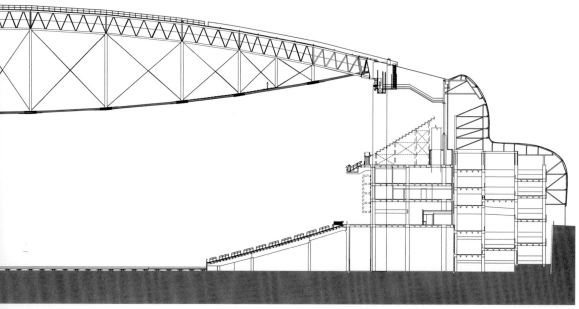

sections, 1:1800

construction documents

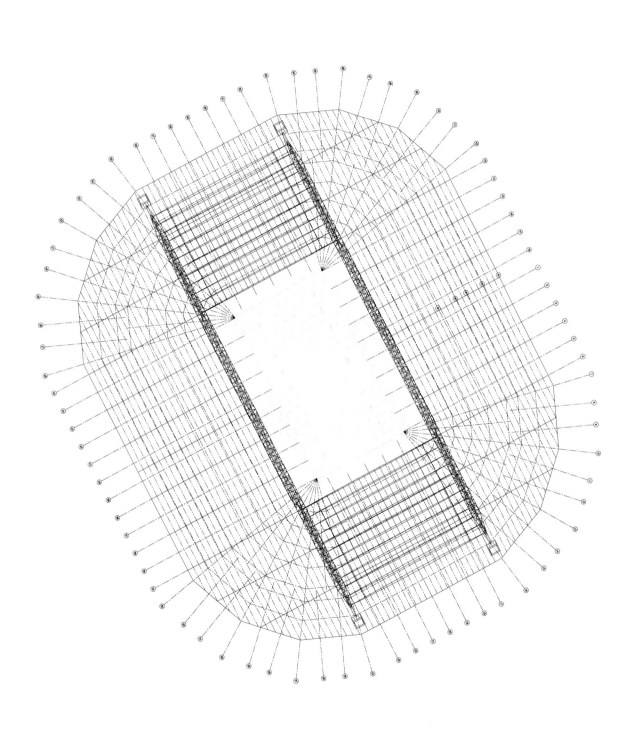

structural roof plan, 1:1800

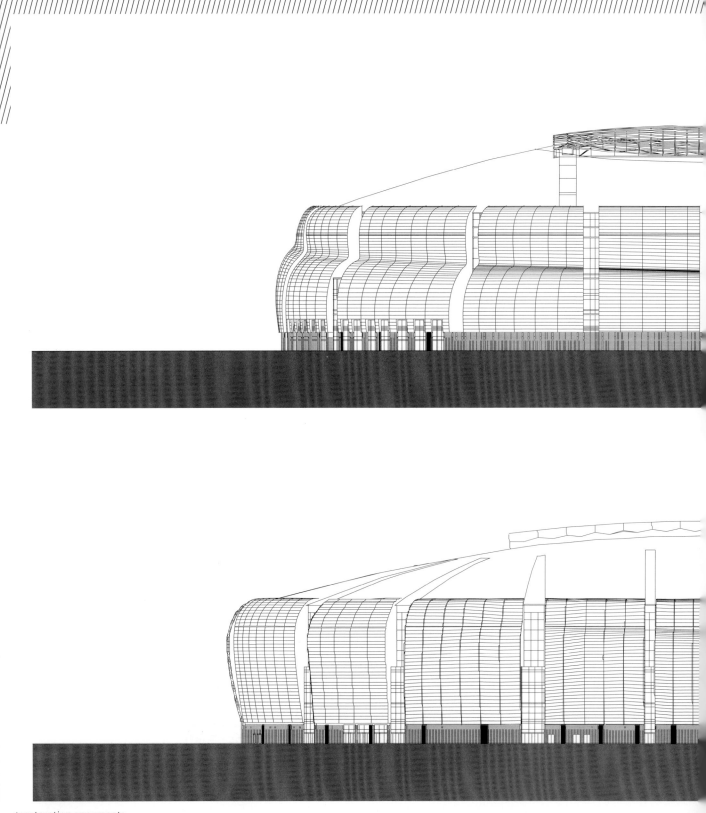

construction documents

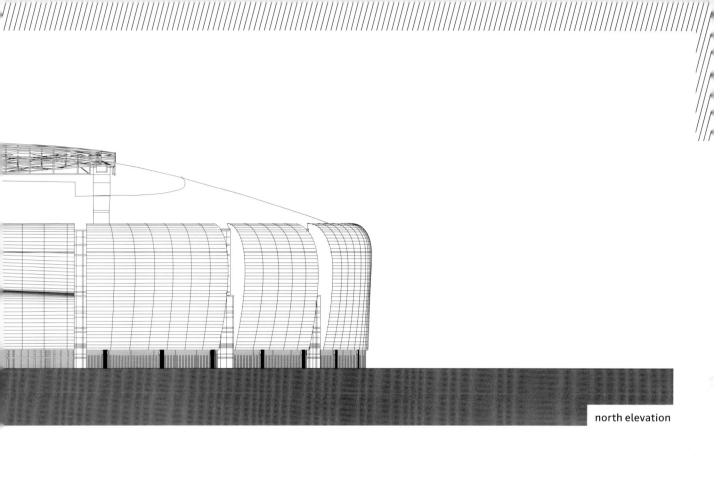

north elevation

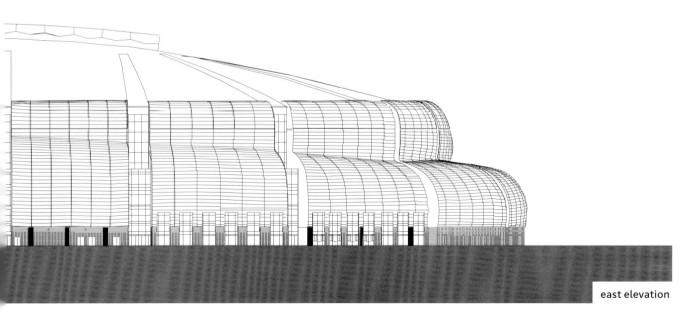

east elevation

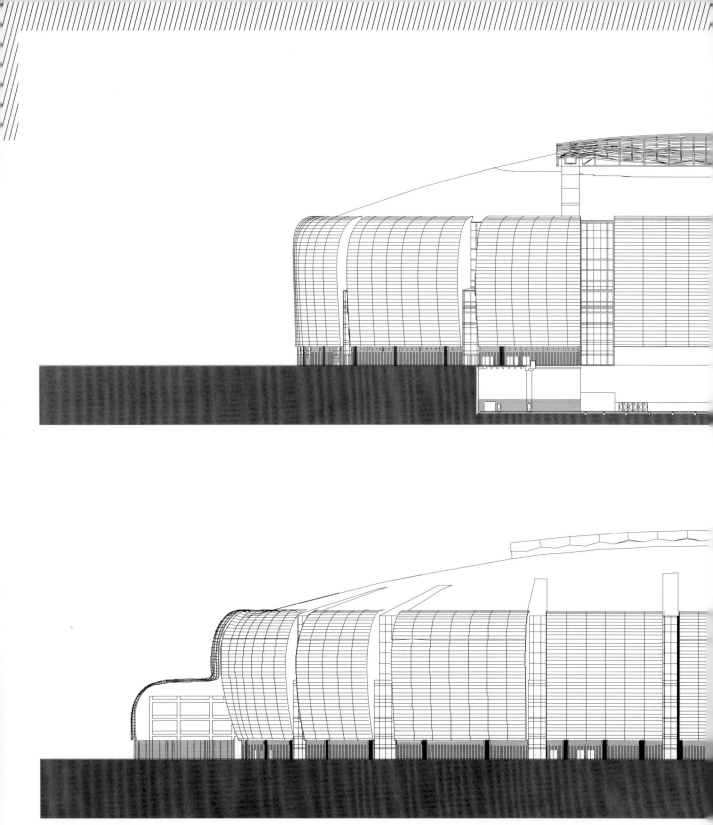

construction documents

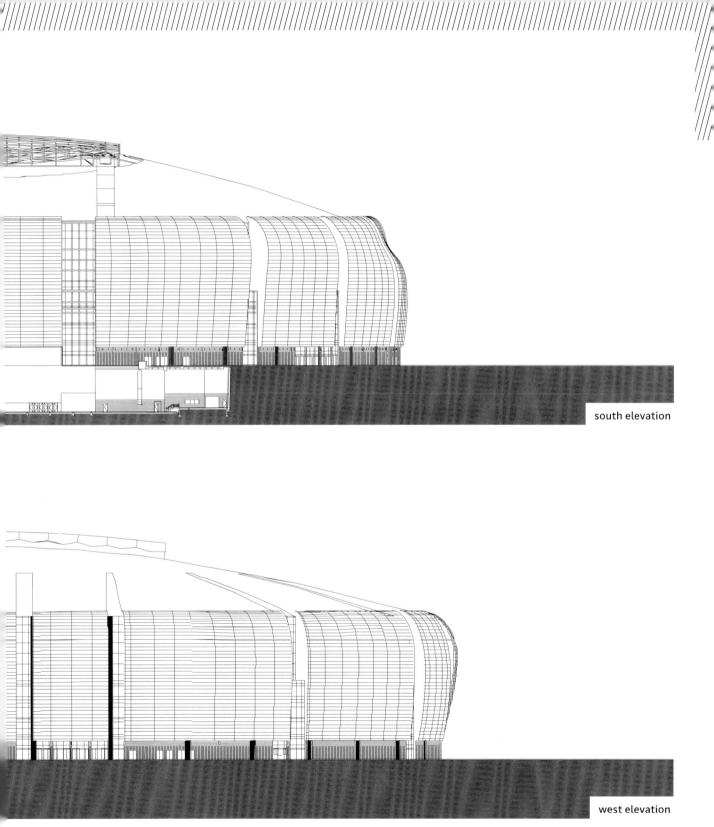
south elevation

west elevation

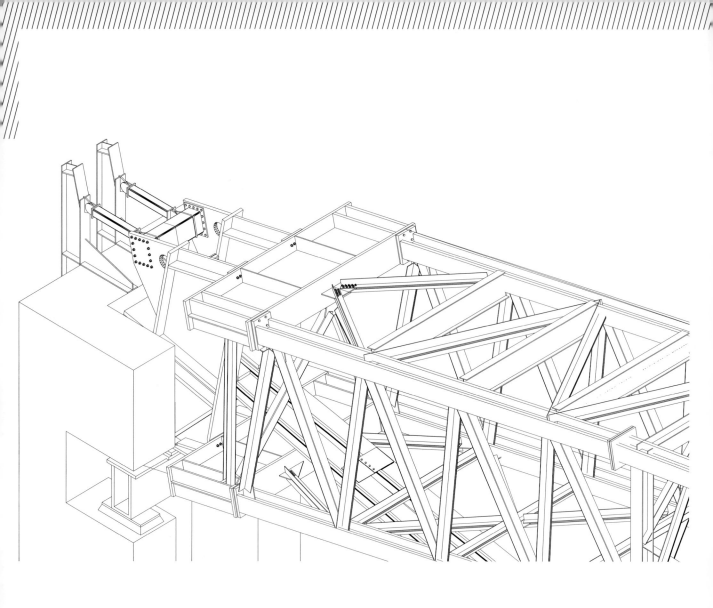

truss detail

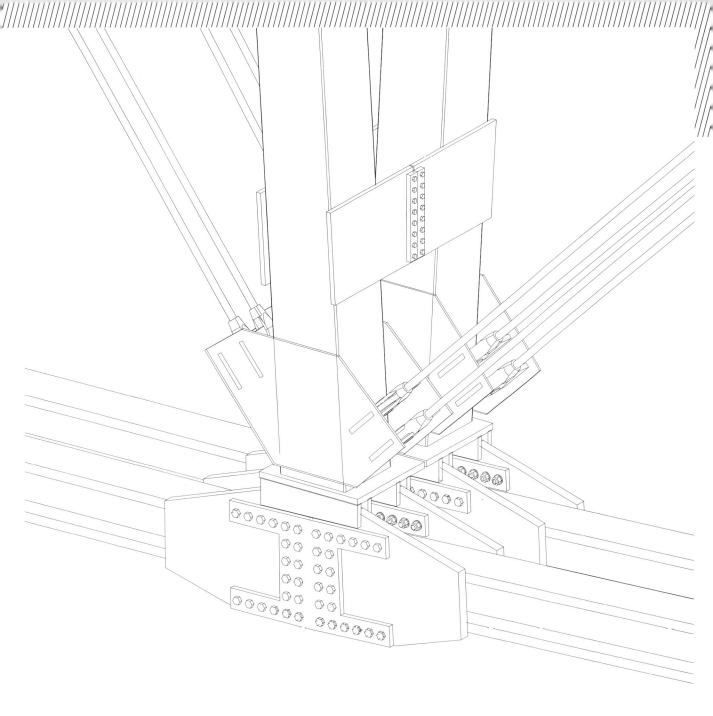

truss detail

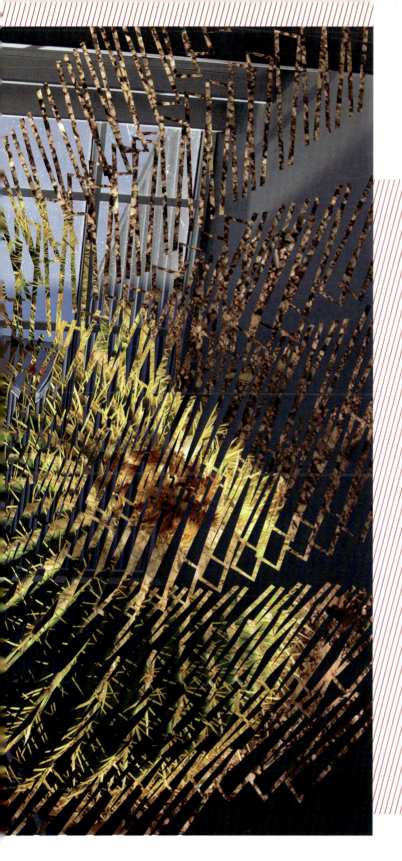

# construction

construction

# concepts, clients, and contractors: building university of phoenix stadium
compiled and edited by todd gannon

PE: Peter Eisenman, principal, Eisenman Architects
RR: Richard Rosson, project architect, Eisenman Architects
TG: Todd Gannon, editor, Source Books in Architecture

**TG: How did your design concepts mesh with the reality of construction?**

RR: When we arrived in Phoenix in 1998, the contractor Hunt Construction Group was already in the room. At first they were an unpaid construction advisor to the Cardinals. Hunt had built many, if not a majority, of the professional sports venues in this country, including the Diamondbacks' Bank One Ball Park [now Chase Field] in downtown Phoenix, so the contractor was already familiar to the Cardinals. Hunt was a local operation. They moved their headquarters to Phoenix from Indianapolis, their home base. Mike Rushman, a Cardinals advisor on financial and design issues, had been the Diamondbacks' lead attorney for the development of Bank One Ball Park.

Hunt was involved in every meeting we had, well before they were hired as the contractor for the project. Hunt placed some constraints on us or, shall we say, they provided guidance. Hunt never said no to anything we proposed. Instead, in a very positive way, they helped us articulate the consequences of our ideas. Their role was not traditional value engineering in the slash-and-burn sense but rather quality, professional construction advice.

PE: There was very little slash and burn.

08.03

08.03

09.03

10.03

12.03

12.03

01.04

01.04

construction

04.06  04.06  04.06  04.06

06.06  06.06  06.06

RR: That's true, and what little that did occur was not Hunt's doing.

TG: **Was the project competitively bid?**

RR: Yes, it had to be because there was public money in the project. But Hunt went into the bidding process with a strong advantage. From the beginning they had strategized not only about how to build the project but how to buy out the project. They became a design-build contractor. We began the project working for the Cardinals, who remained our client until detailed designs were established in order to maintain control of the design process and outcome. Only after working directly with the building architect, landscape architect, and environmental graphic designer did the Cardinals transfer their respective contracts to Hunt, who then was responsible for the completion of working drawings and actual construction.

TG: **At what point was the transition made?**

RR: When Hunt and the Arizona Sports and Tourism Authority (AZSTA) signed an agreement for a Guaranteed Maximum Price on the project, all of the design consultants' contracts shifted to Hunt.

PE: There were moments in that shift when there was talk about removing certain of the consultants.

RR: There was discussion of removing the design architect.

TG: **There is always that discussion.**

RR: Hunt's first move was to sell off major components of the building to subcontractors. For instance, they sold

 05.06

 05.06

 05.06

 05.06

 06.06  06.06

off the fixed and the moving portions of the roof before it was detailed. similarly, they sold off the exterior enclosure before they knew how to build it. They were ultimately responsible for everything being done properly, but they were relieved of the responsibility of figuring out how to build it.

The roof went to a local steel fabricator called Schuff. With Schuff went the structural engineer, W. P. Moore, out of Austin. A company called Crown Corr, from northern Indiana—someone with whom Hunt had worked before—detailed and constructed the enclosure.

PE: They also did our Columbus Convention Center.

RR: Crown Corr assumed responsibility for design and detail drawing as well as for construction, fabrication, and installation.

TG: So Hunt assumed all the responsibility for the project and then immediately started to delegate those responsibilities to various third parties.

RR: Yes, at guaranteed prices.

TG: And this shifted your role from design architect and the owner's primary agent to one among many consultants.

RR: It's false to think we were ever at the top of the pyramid, though we appreciate you thinking that. We were one among many for a number of years. We were there alone at first and then partnered with HNTB as the sports architect. Later, HOK assumed that role. It took some finesse on Hunt's part to get HOK into the project. They are accustomed to being the design architects in sports projects. But, because they had worked with Hunt on so

many sports projects, they agreed to assemble a team of people from their staff. We got along well with the team that they assembled.

As we went through the many iterations of the project, there were many design professionals—a whole battery of people—put into place one layer at a time. Sometimes, as in the case of HNTB, design professionals were creatively removed. At the beginning, we were working with Buro Happold, a structural engineering firm based in Bath, England. When Hunt matched structural designers with fabricators, Buro Happold was paired with an Oklahoma City fabricator. W. P. Moore, who had designed other moving roofs that Hunt had built, was coupled with Schuff. These teams competed to see who would come in with the best price on the two different designs. Schuff was a Phoenix fabricator and W. P. Moore was a known entity—they were always going to get the project. Happold was not. I don't think it was money so much as it was the established reputation of W. P. Moore versus Happold. We wanted Happold, but we didn't have a say—we were lucky even to have Happold at the table. That was Hunt's concession to us.

PE: But the design is pretty close to Happold's original design.

RR: W. P. Moore continued to tinker with their design to make their trusses more slender. At the end of the day, we were pleased with the result.

TG: The question becomes, "How do you pick your battles?" Obviously there is an ambition for authorship, an expectation on the part of the audience that one mind decides everything. But the reality is a complex political struggle. Knowing that there will be more battles than you

construction

have the energy or the ability to fight, how do you choose what to take a stand on and what to give up?

RR: That the Cardinals came to us was a good sign that they wanted something unique in the sports marketplace. They have been entirely consistent in that goal from the beginning.

On this project, we did what we always do. We try to set priorities. Even before there is a design, we spend a lot of time with the client trying to make our design priorities their design priorities. From day one, we agreed that we would create a unique venue.

The Cardinals' priority was their fan base and selling tickets. They and their fans had spent too many hot Sunday afternoons in Sun Devil Stadium, so the Cardinals wanted to put a roof on this thing.

So we said, "Fine, but you've got to crack this thing open, because in the winter you do want to be able to see outside. You want the nice air to come in." That is where the moving roof came from. At one time, one end-zone wall opened, and you really felt like you were outdoors. By opening the wall, the unique aspects of the Phoenix environment came in. The moveable field followed right on that—you couldn't have a natural grass field indoors.

All of these ideas were present at the first site in Tempe, before the project was moved to its present location. There, the stadium opened to the north to Camelback Mountain, which you can see in all of our early renderings. The Bidwills, who were really our client, loved it, because you could see the desert—the landscape was an extension of the stadium interior. This made it unique from Houston and Detroit and from every other stadium that has a roof. They originally wanted air conditioning, but they came to want this openness to the outdoors. These discussions fixed the opening of the stadium roof as a priority for both Eisenman Architects and for the Cardinals. It was never discussed again. But the specifics of these elements were discussed quite a bit. We knew there was a limit to what we could

construction

do with the "vanilla" of the stadium, and in some cases compromises were made. The glazed areas in the facade were reduced; the opening wall was eliminated. But as much as possible, we worked to make our priorities their priorities.

PE: We lost some fights.

RR: Yes, but we won some things. And this was by working with HOK and with the client. HOK could come in and pin six different bowl sections up on the wall. They had a catalog of options. Having sat in a lot of football games, we had an opinion about which of their schemes made the most sense. HOK has two models of concourse design. One has the concessions inboard, the other has them pushed outboard.

We wanted them outboard—the concourses should open to the field. We insisted on the section that was built.

One of the pieces we had to fight for was the slots in the skin. We had to fight HOK for them, because they crimped the floor space for toilets and concessions, and they produce an asymmetrical plan. As the plan of the stadium unfurls around the field, each of the vertical slots becomes a different width. HOK typically designs one quadrant of a football stadium and then builds four of them. But since this plan isn't symmetrical, their standard components had to be adjusted in order to be integrated into our concept. As such, much more documentation was required.

These cuts in the skin emanate from the center of the stadium. They were to come out into the site as plantings and walkways to break up the sea of asphalt. They also were intended to slice through the roof. As it was ultimately built, there is just a ghost of their geometry as markings in the roof with a different color roofing material. That is a battle we fought and lost.

PE: It is important to understand that we didn't lose them because of the budget.

RR: Our original design for this stadium was in Tempe, directly in the flight path of Sky Harbor Airport. The project was stopped after 9-11, and we were forced to locate a new site and start over. But when we got to Glendale, the roof steel had already been ordered. The design drawings were completed. The stadium was under construction. When we changed sites, we had to change the skin design, but everyone was under the gun to get started quickly. An enormous amount of time had been lost in the new site search. When we introduced this design, which included the cuts in the roof, the structural engineer said it would take six or eight weeks of additional design time. There was an incidental material cost involved, but the cost wasn't the issue. Nobody wanted to slow down the process. The Cardinals decided that it wasn't worth it to them.

The stadium has a perforated roof deck for acoustical purposes. You could see a man walking two hundred feet up in the air across this deck, which was fascinating. As is often the case, the deck was going on in a patchwork fashion. Just before the deck was fully closed in, you could see slots in

construction

construction

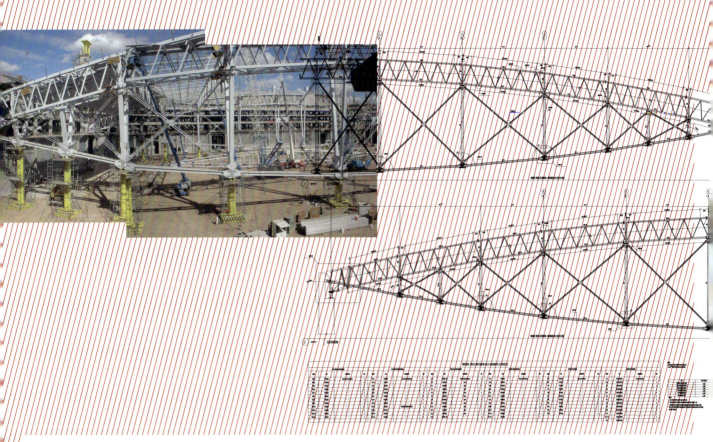

it—not exactly where we had placed the slots, but openings nonetheless. The client and the contractor would go in and say, sheepishly, "Is this what you had in mind for the slots?" and we said, "That's exactly what we had in mind."

TG: There are many wonderful moments that occur during construction, just as there are many wonderful things a client sees through the design process.

In any design project, it is crucial not only to get your client to be truly committed to the concept but also to get them to stop shopping for new ideas. How do you keep them focused on the concept?

RR: You are right, there is always a little bit of that. When a client comes to us, they know they are going to get something that is absolutely unique. If they look at our body of work, there is no repetition at all. Not in design, not in building types—we had never designed a stadium before. They made that decision, not us. When they came to us, they knew that they were in for a different sort of experience. From the start, they wanted something unique from us. Peter and I spend a great deal of time reinforcing that, in assuring the client that they did the right thing when they retained us in the first place. It can get a little bumpy. A client can see something, or the contractor sees something, or the first cost estimate arrives. Sometimes they question whether they made the right choice. I don't think the Cardinals ever questioned these things.

PE: No. The Cardinals never wavered in their support of us, even with the cuts in the roof.

RR: It was an amazing experience. We had day-to-day contact with Hunt, with Crown Corr, with HOK. And the team HOK put on the project really did their best to work with us.

109

construction

Roof Lift: February 18–21, 2006

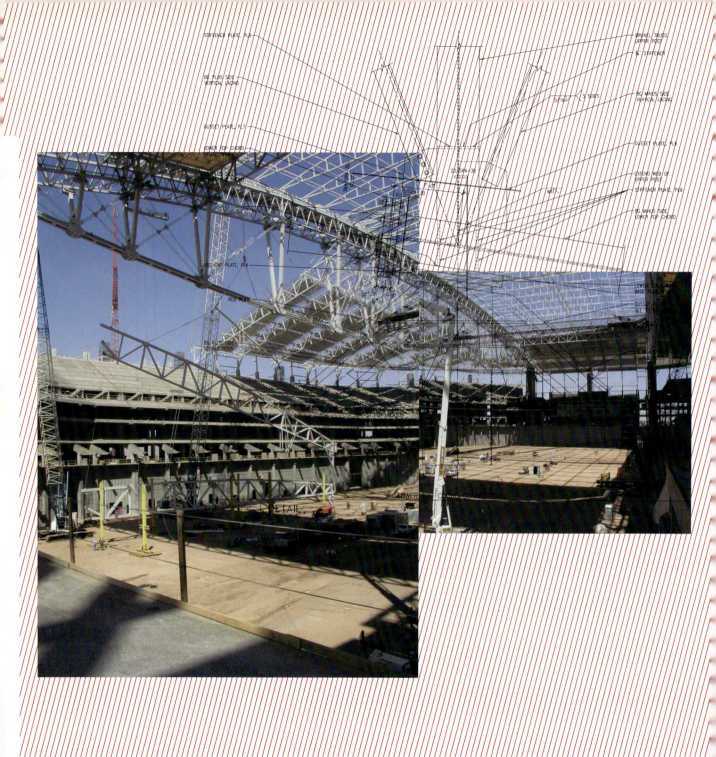

construction

TG: Every one of the exterior panels is different?

RR: Yes. They are a two-inch insulated sandwich panel by Centria, three feet tall and thirty feet wide. They have a kind of tongue-and-groove joint between them. They are flat panels, but it's not a flat skin. The stadium is not symmetrical about any axis. It is spinning out in this snake shape. The curve is different in each of these panels, both in plan and in section.

TG: Given the structural tolerances on that secondary steel, how much play did you have?

RR: Crown Corr, specifically Rich Peller, bought into the notion of making this skin out of metal. He didn't know exactly how he was going to do it at the beginning. When he put his price tag of $23 million on it, he said, "We'll figure it out." We worked closely with him to develop a solution. Financially, there is no way you could custom fabricate every

panel on this building—you just couldn't do it. This is a problem we bump into all the time.

In terms of per-square-foot cost, this is an inexpensive skin. It's $2 per square foot or something. Early on, we realized that it is somewhat forgiving. Over a twenty-foot length, a man could actually twist this panel just enough to give us the kind of curvature that we were looking for.

TG: Were you doing full-scale mockups to figure out how much twist you could afford?

RR: Rich did that in his shop. At first, we were in his office talking about how to make the curved surface. He called back to the shop and said, "Hey Pete. Go get a twenty-foot length of insulated panel. Bolt one end down, and see how far you can twist the other end." In an hour and a half, the guy called back and said, "two-and-a-half to three inches." Pete asked, "How did you do it? Did you set a forklift down on it?" "No," he said, "I just did it with my hands. I figured that you were installing this someplace and it had to be something that a man could do."

TG: How are these twists accommodated on site?

construction

RR: The secondary steel comes off the concrete columns of the stadium—essentially it becomes vertical trusses. They have a rough shape to them. There are horizontal struts that span from one truss to the other, and on that there is a tertiary system of steel. On that, there are clip angles with slotted fittings that allowed them to be adjusted as construction proceeded.

TG: Was that an off-the-shelf clip angle or was that something fabricated specifically for this project?

RR: These were custom clips, part of the miscellaneous metals package. All of it was in Crown Corr's contract.

PE: They had to get a special rig to install these things. There was only one available in the country.

TG: How much direct input did you have here? Did Jerome Scott take the lead in getting this accomplished?

RR: No. Crown Corr had to satisfy Eisenman Architects.

TG: Was that through a performance specification that you provided?

RR: We don't write specifications.

construction

construction

TG: That is an interesting problem then. In the absence of specs, how do you control the project? How do you get these contractors to agree to fixed maximum prices?

RR: We typically no longer do specs or technical drawings. Over the years we have—at the Wexner Center we did 50 percent of the construction documents, for the Aronoff Center in Cincinnati we did 50 percent as well. But it's no fun. We have come to tailor this office to do the things that we are good at doing and that we enjoy doing. Could we hire a spec writer? Yes.

PE: Have we? Yes.

TG: Well, if the spec is one of the customary devices by which architects maintain some leverage in the bidding process, how do you maintain that position?

RR: I'll tell you exactly. If we had a staff of fifty or sixty people, we'd be spending our time managing those fifty or sixty people. We don't have that, which allows us to spend more time in Santiago or in Phoenix or wherever, keeping an eye on things. It's all about relationships. The owners

have to be reassured that they are doing the right thing; the contractors have to be patted on the back. we spend a lot of time establishing personal relationships.

Hunt is one of the good guys. I don't think we have worked with a contractor who is quite as interested in doing a good job as Hunt was. we got eighty-five percent of what we wanted in this design.

TG: Look at landmark projects over the last twenty years. Trace them from schematic design through to the finished building and tally up the losses. Eighty-five percent is through the roof as a batting average.

RR: If you look at the schematic design renderings of this project and look at the finished product, other than the slots in the roof, it's almost identical.

PE: It's almost incredible.

New York City, February 2007

# the stadium

the stadium

the stadium

the stadium

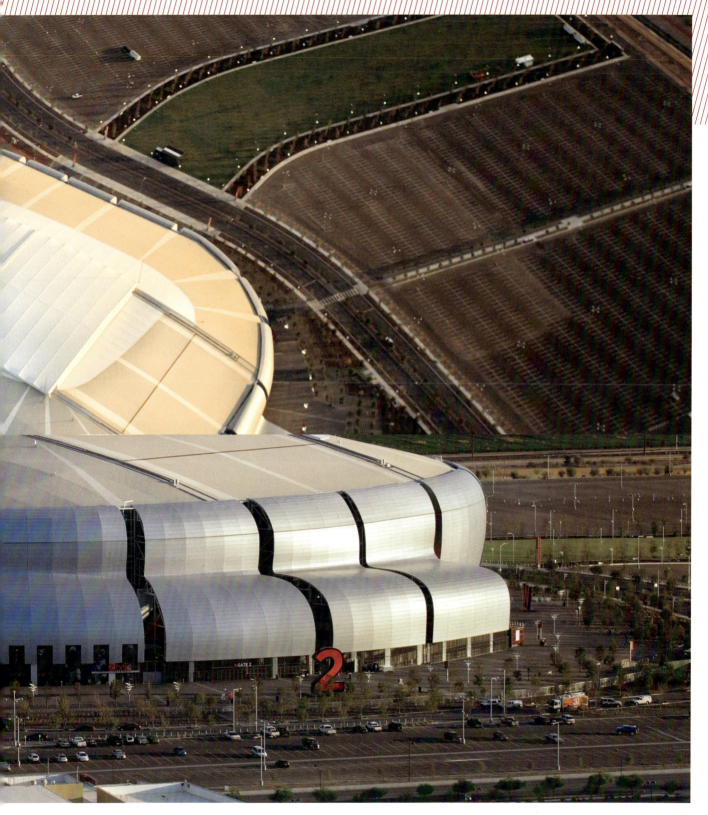

the stadium

the stadium

the stadium

the stadium

the stadium

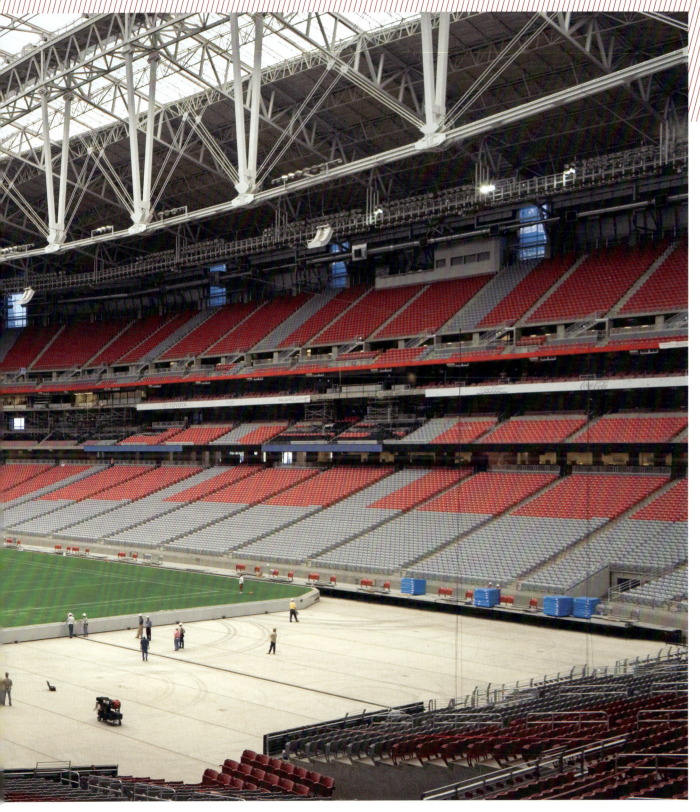

the stadium

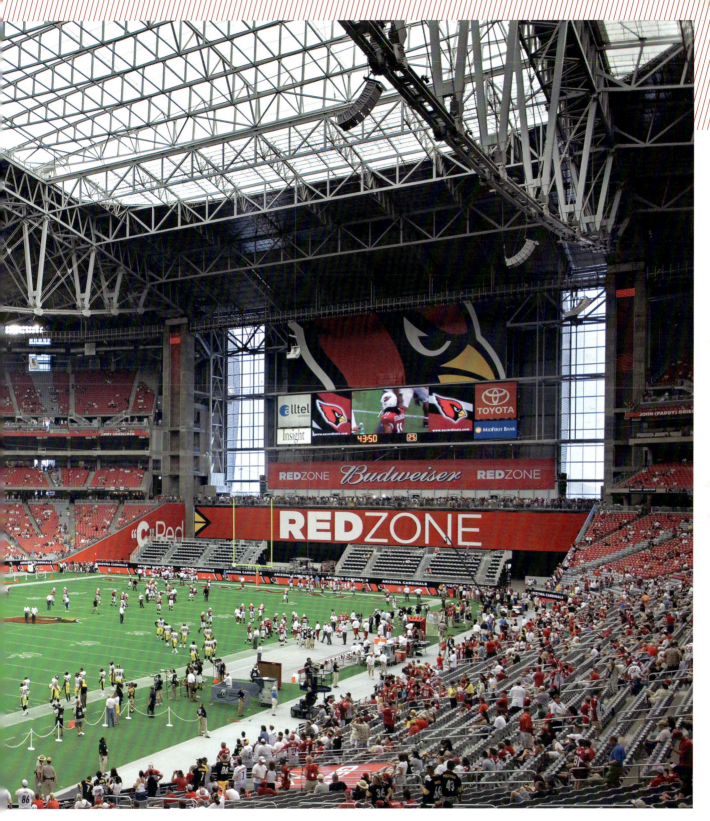

when the big red team takes the field: Jeffrey Kipnis

when the big red team takes the field: Jeffrey Kipnis

Like Minerva springing from the head of Jupiter a fully formed goddess clad in a suit of armor, the professional sports stadium was born a perfected building type. On the day that Emperor Titus opened the Colosseum almost two thousand years ago, the citizens of Rome found eighty numbered gates to facilitate entry and exit, fifty thousand reserved seats separated into different prices based on the quality of view, an interior mall of food services, a retractable sun shade, and an extraordinary infrastructure of "backstage" facilities to serve the athletes and games. The Colosseum provided so excellent a prototype that nothing much has changed in the configuration of the stadium as such in two millennia. The few significant changes that have occurred trace to new technologies—from steel to loud speakers to Fieldturf—while the creative work of the architect remains limited to the stadium's exterior. In fact, no other kind of building has evolved so little over the same course of time, suggesting that the professional sports stadium may rightly claim to be the first building type.

In the parlance of the discipline of architecture, building type refers to any structure whose dominant architectural attributes are predestined by its use, subordinating design discretion to matters of style and taste. The notion of a building type reinforces the common assumption that the architecture of a building is determined by its program, and most professional architects today practice accordingly by specializing in schools, hospitals, office buildings, and even stadiums. Interestingly, however, the discipline of architecture is for the most part not constituted as a catalog of knowledge about building types but as an accumulation of intelligence on the effects of form and formal relations and the behavior of materials. Architects are trained to think in terms like symmetry, composition, hierarchy, courtyards, free-plans, structure, facade, rustication, and transparency far more than in terms of museums, schools, or hospitals.

For those familiar with Peter Eisenman, any discussion of the new stadium in Glendale, Arizona, cannot help but begin by noticing a certain irony. On the one hand, he is a consummate football (and fútbol) nerd—the kind who memorizes players' names and life stories, collects jerseys, and intones fight-song lyrics from high schools and colleges large and small, all to the rolling groan he uses to approximate singing. So who better, then, to design a football stadium? On the other hand, his life's work has amounted to a sustained indictment of a society ever more inclined to the escapist gratifications of diversion than to the deeper felicities of reflection on the arts.

For nearly half a century, Eisenman has staged this critique by using arcane manipulations of architectural form to refute the hackneyed values inherent in the building type: trite pleasures, bourgeois indulgences, and symbolic clichés. Over that period, he has designed intriguing buildings that have worked quite well as houses, schools, museums, and convention centers. But because his formal processes inevitably run afoul of the rote conventions of the building type, these structures also provide his clients and audience with as much provocation for reflection as a work of philosophy or criticism. Of course, it does mean that some strange things show up, like a column in the middle of a master bedroom or an upside-down staircase. These exotica are never mere whims but isolated features within a sustained discussion about contemporary life that plays out throughout the design as a whole.

Given that escapist entertainment is the sine qua non of the sports stadium and considering the inflexibility of it as a building type (just imagine a column in front of your fifty-yard line seat simply to make you think!), what is Eisenman to do? With his architectural discretion limited to the exterior, he is unable to craft the project into another of his studies in architecture-as-critical-essay. So, he changes genre, from the essay to the poem, seeking an attitude apposite to contemporary architectural poetry that might parallel his essays' native bent toward criticality.

Then the architect joins the big red team of collaborators, engineers, and consultants to dispatch the requisite demands. As expected, they enhance custom and accommodation with

when the big red team takes the field: Jeffrey Kipnis

new technology, evidenced in the much-heralded operative field tray and the retracting roof supported on two giant Brunel trusses. Meanwhile, Eisenman and his inner circle begin to write, and after seven drafts tender a single agreeable, if slightly awkward, stanza, a rondelet of sorts.

Its dominant features are a simple, pug-nosed oval sliced into sections, each surfaced in high metallic sheen, and an incongruous furrow half-circumscribing the overall form. Like most poems, it poses no real challenges;[1] it is easy to ignore and few will pay little more attention to it than to recognize it as kind of modern with a twist. But neither does the stadium indulge the tendency toward the fantastic found in such fan-oriented stadiums as Herzog and de Meuron's exciting Allianz Arena in Munich, Germany, which changes colors during night games to broadcast the team colors and then display the emotional ebb and flow of the game within. In that sense, the audience for Eisenman's architecture is less the fan of games than those few in Glendale/Phoenix inclined to reflect on it at a distance, over time and independent of its program.

A [wikipedia](#) entry recounts the allusions the architect professes to offer this audience, and, after one learns of them, its poesy becomes palpable:

when the big red team takes the field: Jeffrey Kipnis

The facility is supposed to resemble a barrel cactus with a coiled rattlesnake around it...Looking down on the stadium, there is a Native-American design, or "mandala," on the roof which is repeated on the seats inside. The rays of the design radiate out 21 different vertical glass slots [that] represent the unique "slot canyons" found in northern Arizona and southern Utah. The metal skin of the stadium reflects the changing quality of light in the Arizona skies. The stadium starts out each morning with a light golden color, takes on more of a silver-blue tone during the day and finishes up with pinks, oranges, and purples during sunset.[2]

Given these regional sentiments, why does the building look and feel alien in a context surfeited with regional sensitivity under the influence of Frank Lloyd Wright? Everywhere in greater Phoenix, buildings "respond" to the desert with local stone, rust-hued stucco, or Exterior Insulation Finish Systems (EIFS), low-slung flat roofs, and Indian-themed ornaments and rock gardens à la Taliesen West. And in truth, casual observers will instinctively associate the stadium not with the indigenous Southwest but with the only other significant architectural idiom in the area, the innocuous crop of modern corporate high rises and institutional buildings that provide some respite from the city's cloying carpet of routine good intentions.

when the big red team takes the field: Jeffrey Kipnis

Nor are they wrong. Eisenman's design alludes to a species of architectural modern that belongs neither to the Platonic absolute of glass-and-steel geometry nor to Wright's organicism. Aloof, diffident, it communicates reluctantly with its relatives. It proposes no new order and, in fact, chafes at any acquiescence to a dominant order, whether as profound as Wright's or as banal as corporate modernism.

To move the stadium toward this species of modern, Eisenman draws on his earlier work on "weak form," first appearing in the Columbus Convention Center (1989–93). Though derived from the difficult semiotics of indexicality, weak form might best be understood as an architectural analog to a cloud's ability to suggest many figures and partial figures.[3] Though Eisenman first introduced it as a critical tool, the promiscuous ambiguity of weak form makes it a perfect device for poetry. In the stadium, weak form in its original sense is most evident in the furrow that melds snake and cactus into one figure, but the materiality and the sectioning of the oval also contribute to the effect.

Like any poem, the University of Phoenix Stadium rewards readers in proportion to the knowledge and work they bring to its reading. We need to know of the barrel cactus, the rattle snake, the slot canyons, and the mandala, but even that is not enough, for what <u>wikipedia</u> fails to tell us is that these figures are not the meaning of the stadium but, like Poe's bells, merely the tropes the architect uses to make meaning restless and thus invite the deepening of manifold interpretation.

If, as the southwestern figures first suggest, the stadium is a poem about the context, then can its allusion to the ubiquitous car be ignored? It is, after all, a shiny new convertible, and from many vantage points, the furrow and aluminum panels unmistakably echo the familiar door panel inflections of a silver Chevy Malibu or Ford Mondeo. And certainly, the stadium's fourteen-thousand-space parking lot and the highways it connects to are today more indigenous to the area than are relics of Native American tribes.

But the furrow, whose progressive growth and terminal flutter are the most unusual formal feature of the stadium, is the poem's verb, the destabilizing element that is even more evocative in its temporality than its figurality. Does it perhaps anticipate the damage that will occur one day when the roll-in field does not stop as it should and crashes into the opposite side? The pie-cut sections are said to devolve from the slot canyons, and Eisenman has taken care to make sure the spacing between each is different from the other. Still, given the dramatic undulating surfaces of the actual canyons, it is not unreasonable to ponder why the pie-cuts end up so staunch and regimented. Why not render their famous undulating surfaces more faithfully? Doing so would have undermined the mandala

When the Big Red Team Takes the Field: Jeffrey Kipnis

figure on the roof, but, more importantly, abstraction from verisimilitude is the essential first step to set the mind free and put metaphor and metonymy into play. In the spirit of this freedom, it is easy to imagine the assembly of sections as players in a huddle. In the ~~bird's~~ blimp's-eye-view, we see their backs as they bend forward to hear the call, and from a distance at ground level we see that all-too-familiar oval of big muscular butts in shiny skin-tight pants.

In concert with these pie-cut sections, the furrowed surface opens this stadium as no other to musings about the place of professional football in our lives. It is, after all, a temporal event in all of its dimensions, from its plays and seasons to the coming together and scattering of its fans. When we think about it, like the fans, the professional players are complex individuals who come together and voluntarily relinquish their individuality for the pleasure, power, and productivity of participating in a uniform and univocal collective. Does the flutter of the furrow remind us to remember that such passionate phalanxes—whether of players or fans or a nation—are valuable when provisional, but dangerous when permanent?

The term fascism derives from the Roman fascia, which refers to the bundle of sticks bound together with a rope that was the symbol of senatorial power in ancient Rome. One can see the fascia on the back of the old U.S. Mercury dime, alongside the

national motto, E. Pluribus Unum. what is less known is that the Latin term fascia means "a band of cloth worn as a symbol of royalty"—around the head for a man or draped over shoulder and breast for a woman. The ancient senatorial symbol derived its name from the strength of its bindings. In Eisenman's stadium the furrow transforms the steel-paneled surface into an immense fascia that binds the phalanx together, but whether it is tightening or loosening, and which if either of those is desirable, are questions left to the reader. what is certain, however, is that these are the kinds of questions we most need poetry to ask. Few other stadiums since the Roman Colosseum have ever tried.
—Jeffrey Kipnis

## NOTES

1. "Ars Poetica" by Archibald MacLeish (1925)

A poem should be palpable and mute
As a globed fruit
Dumb
As old medallions to the thumb

Silent as the sleeve-worn stone
Of casement ledges where the moss has grown—
A poem should be wordless
As the flight of birds
A poem should be motionless in time
As the moon climbs
Leaving, as the moon releases
Twig by twig the night-entangled trees,
Leaving, as the moon behind the winter leaves,
Memory by memory the mind—
A poem should be motionless in time
As the moon climbs
A poem should be equal to:
Not true
For all the history of grief
An empty doorway and a maple leaf
For love
The leaning grasses and two lights above the sea—
A poem should not mean
But be.

2. http://en.wikipedia.org/wiki/University_of_Phoenix_Stadium

3. Clouds are a changing "record" of complex interactions among air flows of different temperature and humidity. They are neither infinitely variable nor random, falling into predictable types—cumulus, nimbus, cirrus, and stratus—as persistent interactions of airflow repeat themselves. Cumulus and nimbus clouds are the most evocative, and their capacity to suggest so many figures obtains from three features: each cloud is more or less discrete and monotonic, it arises out of an intricate structure of minute interactions that change over time, and the visible record of the interactions is curvilinear.

Eisenman's initial idea for generating weak form architecture was straightforward, even if the actual design techniques required were mind-boggling (and have since been given over to computers): create design processes that cause simple forms to interact with one another over time like the airflows in clouds. For most, the Columbus Convention Center was just another of his inexplicably wacky projects. But those who paid closer attention discovered its uncanny ability to draw so many disparate and disjointed aspects of the surrounds—the expressways, a nearby factory, the local building fabric, and the nearby downtown high rises—into a strange, loose-knit coherence without imposing a new order and without looking like anything else around it. Much has changed in his work in the decade and half since, but the influence of his thought on weak form can be felt in most projects since, including the stadium.

# project credits

| | |
|---|---|
| client: | Arizona Cardinals |
| | Arizona Sports and Tourism Authority |
| Design Builder: | Hunt Construction Group |
| Design Architect: | Eisenman Architects |
| Facility Architect: | HOK Sport |
| Environmental Graphics: | Pentagram Design |
| Design and Interiors: | Entro Communications |
| Project Management: | Land Strategies |
| Construction Management: | N. W. Getz & Associates |
| | Columbus Consulting |
| Landscape Architect: | Urban Earth Design |
| Structural Roof Engineer: | Walter P Moore |
| Structural Frame Engineer: | TLCP Structural Inc. |
| Mech / Electrical Engineer: | M-E Engineers |
| Civil Engineer: | Evans, Kuhn and Associates |
| | CMX Sports Engineers, Inc. |
| Electrical Engineer: | CR Engineers |
| Bridge Engineer: | Stanley Consultants |
| Geotechnical Engineer: | GEC |
| Playing Field: | CMX Sports Engineers |
| Food Service Design: | Cini-Little |
| Code Consultant: | FSC |

## major subcontractors

| | |
|---|---|
| Structural Concrete: | Kiewit Western |
| Precast Concrete: | Kiewit Western |
| Exterior Enclosure: | Crown Corr, Inc. |
| Structural Steel: | Schuff Steel |
| Structural Roof Lift: | Mammoet |
| Roof & Field Mechanization: | Uni-Systems |
| HVAC & Plumbing: | TD Industries |
| Electrical: | Cannon & Wendt |
| | Kimbrell Electric |
| Fire Protection: | Aero Automatic |
| Scoreboards: | Daktronics |
| Audio / Visual Systems: | Pro Sound |
| Telecommunications: | Insight |
| Stadium Seating: | Irwin Seating |
| Playing Field: | Valley Crest |
| Elevators / Escalators: | Kone |
| Fabric Roof: | Taiyo Birdair |
| Masonry: | Sun Valley |
| Steel Stairs & Railings: | Southwest Stair |
| Metal Framing / Drywall: | AROK |
| Graphics: | Fluoresco |
| | GM Nameplate |
| Food Service Equipment: | Baring |
| Interiors: | ISEC |
| Furniture: | Facilitec |
| Grading & Paving: | Markham Construction |
| Plaza Concrete: | Concrete Finishing |
| Site Concrete: | RBG Construction |
| Storm Drainage: | C S & W Construction |
| 95th Ave Bridges: | CS Construction |
| Landscaping: | Valley Crest |
| Water Feature: | Aquatec Fountains |

# Author Bios

**Todd Gannon** is a registered architect and senior associate with Kovac Architects in Los Angeles. A graduate of The Ohio State University, he currently teaches architectural theory and design at Otis College of Art and Design, having previously taught at Ohio State and UCLA. As series editor of Source Books in Architecture, he has published the work of Morphosis, Bernard Tschumi, UN Studio, Steven Holl, Mack Scogin/Merrill Elam, Zaha Hadid, and the MoMA exhibition "Light Construction." His essays have appeared in Log, Loud Paper, Dialogue, and elsewhere. He is currently at work on a dissertation at UCLA focused on the British architectural collaborative Archigram.

After fifteen years as Dean of the College of Architecture and Environmental Design at Arizona State University **John Meunier** devoted a sabbatical year to the study in-situ of desert cities around the world, elaborating an interest in the urban logic of the desert context of his university. While Director of the School of Architecture and Interior Design at the University of Cincinnati, and before that as a faculty member of the School of Architecture at Cambridge University he studied and designed for the very different cultural logics of their urban settings. He has degrees from Liverpool, Cambridge, and Harvard universities.

**Jeffrey Kipnis** is professor of architectural design and theory at the Knowlton School of Architecture of The Ohio State University. His writings on art and architecture have appeared in such publications as Log, Hunch, Harvard Design Magazine, Quaderns, 2G, El Croquis, Art Forum, Assemblage, and his books include Chora L Works: Jacques Derrida and Peter Eisenman, Perfect Acts of Architecture, and The Glass House. As architecture/design curator for the Wexner Center for the Arts, he organized the design survey, "Mood River" with co-curator Annetta Massie, and "Suite Fantastique," a compilation of four exhibitions: Perfect Acts of Architecture, The Furniture of Scott Burton, The Predator – a collaboration between Greg Lynn and Fabian Marcaccio, and Imaginary Forces – Motion Graphics. His film, A Constructive Madness, produced in collaboration with Tom Ball and Brian Neff, looks at the architect's work on the unbuilt but seminal Peter Lewis house project. His most recent study of Steven Holl's Bloch Addition to the Nelson Atkins Museum appears in Holl's new book, Stone and Feather.

**photo credits**

© Arizona Cardinals   18, 20-21, 52-59, 110-111, 144, 148-149

Buro Happold Consulting Engineers, P.C.   33

dbox   16-17, 20, 69, 73-75

Michael Dollin   8-9, 12-13, 16-17, 92-93

Eisenman Architects and HNTB   18, 28, 30-32, 34, 37-39, 41-43,

Eisenman Architects and HOK Sport   72-73, 78, 80-82

Roland Halbe   2, 134-135

HOK Sport   70-71, 83-84, 104

Courtesy of Hunt Construction Group   20, 76-77, 94-99

Construction photos are courtesy of Hunt Construction Group or Eisenman Architects   13, 21, 92-93, 100-109, 112-121

David Sundberg/Esto © Arizona Cardinals   26-27, 60-61, 122-133, 136-141, 152

Walter P Moore   85, 109, 112-115